'*Rashai*', th
ingly, appa
know the
'minister', h
second syllable which rhymes with 'sky', for I had stressed the first.

Steve, an American, was most people's idea of a typical Gypsy. With a tanned complexion and black moustache, he had the most arresting, brilliant dark eyes I had ever seen. His smile seemed to approve the title I had assumed and I believe it to be apt. Strong as my interest in Gypsy education and general welfare may be, fascinated as I am to study their native tongue, it is with religious life, especially the remarkable current revival that I am most concerned. So '*rashai*', 'minister,' I am and if, thinking of me, the Gypsies are thereby helped to think of their Lord I will be happy.

Travelling Home

God's work of revival among Gypsy folk

JOE RIDHOLLS

Marshall Pickering

Dedicated to my four grandchildren:
Laura, Thomas, Samuel and Amy
and any more who may appear!

Marshall Morgan and Scott
Marshall Pickering
3 Beggarwood Lane, Basingstoke, Hants RG23 7LP, UK

First published in 1986 by Marshall Morgan and Scott
Publications Ltd
Part of the Marshall Pickering Holdings Group
A subsidiary of the Zondervan Corporation

British Library Cataloguing in Publication Data

Ridholls, Joe
Travelling home.
1. Gypsies——Religious life 2. Christian
life——1960–
I. Title
248.8 BV4501.2

ISBN 0–551–01351–6

Phototypeset in Linotron Plantin by
Input Typesetting Ltd, London SW19 8DR
Printed in Great Britain by
HazellWatson & Viney Ltd, Aylesbury, Bucks.

Contents

Romany Chorus

Trav'lling, Jesus kept trav'lling, no home to live in, just like a Romany.
Struggling never to give in, scorned and despised but living free.
That's why He hears our sighing, on Him relying we will travel on.
Follow, Lord we will follow, until our lifelong journey's done.
Onward, Jesus pressed onward, seeking the lost and outcasts in Galilee.
Never counting the cost, and helping the helpless to be free.
We'll give Him our affection, take the direction that his word will show
Follow, Lord we will follow, Romany pilgrims here below.
Forward, Jesus moved forward, leaving the living, dying on Calvary.
Freely His pardon giving, rising again to victory.
Now His Spirit is blowing, God's purpose showing for the Romany.
Follow, Lord we will follow Jesus who died to set us free.

Words by Joe Ridholls (Rashai)
Music by Kenneth Pelmear

Introduction

In just over thirty years of the Gypsy revival about 70,000 Gypsies have become converted and baptised, and more than 300,000 attend their evangelical meetings. 1,600 Gypsy men have become preachers, 400 of whom are now pastors, and an army of preachers awaits the opportunity to take the message of the Christian gospel to the twenty million or more Gypsies (excluding those in India) who still do not know Christ.

As I have, over the years, tried to trace the progress of this remarkable religious movement, and as my reactions to it have varied, it has always, in the last analysis, left me moved, impressed and rebuked. Imperfect though it undoubtedly is ('we have this treasure in earthen vessels') I have never ceased to be amazed at the greatness of the power of God it so clearly reveals. Looking, in contrast, at the present state of much of the Christianity of the West, I am often tempted to quote an old Methodist hymn which asks the question: 'And shall we ever live at this poor, dying rate?' Certainly too, I have been impressed and even shamed by the lively and highly successful evangelistic efforts, over many years and in several countries, of the French Gypsy evangelists under the apostolic leadership of Clément Le Cossec, a Breton Pentecostalist of non-Gypsy origins. If revival does not come when we want, pray for it as we may, there is surely a salutary lesson to be learnt from the dedicated, ceaseless 'pushing' (to use a favourite Le Cossec expression) of evangelism. The revival and evangelism depicted in this book is specialised inasmuch as it is almost entirely confined to the Gypsy race, and there can be no doubt that their very tribal structure, its psyche affected deeply by God's action, has contributed in no small way to its success. The very fact of its success however, even allowing for this factor, shows what God can do today if we are faithful in presenting His gospel.

I will attempt to describe how the revival started and grew, first in France and then in Spain and other countries of Western Europe. We will follow its remarkable progress to parts of the world like Scandinavia, North and South America and finally, through the countries of Eastern Europe, right back into India, the land from which the Gypsies first came. But first I should explain how I personally became involved in the work of Gypsy revival.

ONE

A glimpse of the fire

'They won't touch you if you don't move.' The Gypsy boy watched me, a mischievous grin on his face. He knew I was scared. I'm not exactly the world's greatest dog-lover and to be surrounded by a circle of vicious-looking lurchers was not my idea of a good time. 'What will happen if I do move?' I asked him hesitantly. 'They'll have your leg off,' he assured me, grinning more than ever. As I moved, they moved, the circle slowly, menacingly closing. Then, blessed relief, he called them off and I could breathe again!

I had met the boy several weeks previously, the very day, in fact, on which I arrived at Pool in Cornwall to begin my work as a minister in the Camborne Circuit of the Methodist Church; this was in September 1975. We had taken a break from unpacking to get something to eat and, on my way to buy some fish and chips, I had got into conversation with an elderly man. You don't unpack a removal lorry with your 'dog-collar' on, and he did not know who I was. As we stood and passed the time of day three young boys passed us. The man pointed dramatically to them and, in a stage whisper, said, 'You see them? They're wolves!' They were in fact Gypsy boys from a local encampment and, leaving him to his prejudices, I hurried after them and introduced myself. Fortunately when I subsequently went up to the camp and found myself surrounded by the dogs it was one of these boys, who, after enjoying my plight for a little while, had rescued me.

I had intended to visit that site, known as Boscarne Park, up on the bleak Carn Brea hill, even before I had arrived in the area. Never before had I lived near to so many Gypsies and, receiving the local paper before my actual arrival in the area, I had learnt of their existence and had resolved to try to get to know them. It was the presence of the dogs that had made me hesitate for a while, but finally I said, 'Lord, if you want me to go up, keep the dogs away!' I thought to myself now that the Lord, if He hadn't exactly answered my earlier prayer, had at least worked in a very effective way.

Like most people, of course, I had had some contact with Gypsies. Like George Borrow in his *Gypsies of Spain*, I could say, 'Throughout my life the Gypsy race has always had a particular interest for me,' and I had found all previous contacts with them fascinating. I had met Gypsies in the Welsh Border country and remember particularly the large, formidable Gypsy woman, broken nose, pipe in mouth, who would embarrass me severely whenever she saw me from afar. 'He's a nice young man, he is,' she would announce to all and sundry, 'believes in God Almighty, he does!' From Pedro, the little Gypsy boy I once taught in Yorkshire to the Gypsy girls who took advantage of a youth meeting in my house in Cambridgeshire to have a bath, they had been, to say the least, unconventional and never uninteresting! Now I had a real chance to get to know them better and, as a Christian minister, to try to reach them with the gospel. But how do you start? You just go to the site, I decided, and this was what I had done.

The direct approach paid off. Week after week I visited them, got to know their names, drank tea in their trailers, seeking to disarm their deeply-rooted (and not totally unjustified) suspicions until eventually I was accepted at a certain level. They called me 'Father Joe' sometimes but gradually it became 'Jose', short for

Joseph (itself a popular name with them), and I felt I had made real contact but only up to a certain point. That point was passed when I first spoke at a Gypsy funeral.

Teresa Isaacs had died and the funeral service was to take place in the Parish Church at Illogan, near Pool. When I approached the vicar, with whom I worked quite closely and very happily, he was only too pleased for me to give the address. A Gypsy funeral is a never-to-be-forgotten experience. They will turn up in their hundreds, spend a fortune on flowers – often filling two open lorries, as well as the hearse, with imaginative floral tributes. At the graveside everyone throws in a handful of earth and the mourners display great grief and emotion.

As I stood up in that church to speak I saw a congregation of perhaps 200 Gypsies. Men, women and children of every age range, they were vigorous, emotional and intensely aware of family and race. I experienced what I can only describe as a feeling of deep love for them. If only, I thought to myself, if only God could get hold of them, what Christians they would make! How it would spread! As I look back I believe this was indeed the prompting of the Holy Spirit, who was to show me how God was in fact getting hold of Gypsy folk as never before in history.

What could I say to help them in their grief? I spoke of the sun that rises to warm the slopes of the Carn, the hill on which they live. At the end of the day, I pointed out to them, it would set at last into the sea, leaving behind it a warm, red afterglow. So, I told them, it was with Teresa. Her life, in its noonday, had brought life and warmth to them and now, in her passing, the bright, warm afterglow of her memory still lingered on. Up to the time when I rose to speak they had been crying loudly, even through the singing of the hymns which, as they were unable to read, they could not sing. Beforehand I had been quite concerned about their possible behaviour during my address. In fact they sat in complete and very attentive silence. When at last I finished and stepped back for the vicar to close the service, the widower, old Matt Isaacs, got to his feet and shouted 'Thank you sir, that was handsome, beautiful, beautiful!' I went with them to the graveside and, casting a handful of earth into the grave, felt anew this sense of love, of affinity. Certainly this was a contact deeper than I had made before. Little though did I realise that, within a matter of weeks, I would be back with them in an hour of grief even more poignant.

One of the several grandsons of Matt and his late wife Teresa was Bobby Isaacs. By any standards he was a fine youngster. Fourteen years of age, he was captain of cricket, soccer and rugby at the local school. Several times I had been swimming with him and some of the other boys and he and my own son had become quite friendly. What, however, was not known was that Bobby, athletic as he appeared to be, had a heart defect. On the very eve of the school rugby team's departure for a tour of Wales he suddenly dropped dead. His family was shattered, especially his mother and father, Nellie and Joe. Again I was asked to speak at a Gypsy funeral. As the coffin was carried into the church, with wreaths in the form of a cricket bat and a rugby ball, I felt I shared their grief and, for the only time whilst conducting a funeral, I felt tears running down my own cheeks. I compared Bobby to a shooting star that passes briefly and brilliantly over the night sky, something they would have often seen. I felt it was all very inadequate but later I discovered that they remembered these word-pictures and I knew that a still deeper contact had been made.

We tried to maintain this contact in a variety of ways. We started a youth club for Gypsies, and students from the Cornwall Technical College and School of Mines came to help. What would the Gypsies make of Fred, I wondered? He was known as Fred because his real Nigerian name was too much of a mouthful. Would they resent a Negro? Indeed not, they loved him as he helped in the club along with a few of the local people.

I'm no stranger to youth work but these Gypsies were totally unclubbable! They couldn't stay in one activity for more than a few moments at a time and were never happier than when they were running around or fighting on the floor! At least though, we were gaining their confidence, although there were times when we felt close to abandoning the whole thing. Then we received timely practical encouragement. Prince Charles is Duke of Cornwall as well as Prince of Wales and there was a Prince's Fund administered through a local trust who worked mainly with needy children. From them we obtained £200.

Now we could expand our activities. If you can't cope with Gypsy children indoors, then take them out. I was able to take them playing five-a-side football, skate-boarding and swimming at the local leisure centre, all getting-to-know-you processes of pre-evangelism. For I was now beginning to feel that the time was approaching for a more specifically evangelistic approach. They had attended some services, it was true; some had come sporadically to Sunday School; a few babies had been christened; but now something different was needed. What I really wanted was a group of young Christians to come and live at the local chapel and conduct a mission among the Gypsies.

I knew some of the members of the Christian Union of Westminster College, Oxford, which is a Methodist Teachers' Training College and, when I approached them with this suggestion, they readily and very enthusi-astically agreed to come. It was to be Easter 1977, and a team of them led by David Easton, a Cornishman who was teaching nearby (he had been President of the College Union and is now a Methodist Minister), came to live for a week or so in the schoolrooms of the chapel. How they worked and how the Gypsies loved them! Games, activities indoors and out of doors, services, choruses, barbecues, — they did the lot! So greatly did they gain the Gypsies' confidence and lively friendship that their greatest difficulty was to get any privacy or free time, so popular did they become.

One evening was a disaster though. A combination of events revealed some aspects of Gypsy psychology that we had not previously suspected. There was a barbecue and some local Methodist youth workers were invited. It had seemed a good idea but we had made a great mistake. We had not realised that the Gypsies loved the students with all the deep, passionate and very jealous love of their ardent natures. Never before had a group of people taken so personal, practical and Christian an interest in them. They were their students, nobody else's. 'We don't want those other ——', they objected vociferously and they expressed their opposition by going on a rampage which we just could not control, and which left us all shattered, sad and very discouraged at the end of the day. The students, disconsolate, were just about getting off to sleep very late that night when they heard the noise of some people coming up the hill towards the chapel. It was the Gypsies! What would happen? The Gypsy youngsters stayed outside and wailed and mourned aloud in sheer remorse for what they had done that evening! We all learnt a lot that day.

Some of the Gypsy youngsters were sincerely moved by the Christian witness of the students; they still sing the choruses they were taught and a necessarily one-sided correspondence has been maintained ever since. The day the students were due to go they came to see me because they were unable to leave. The Gypsies, heartbroken at their departure and trying to delay it as long as possible, had taken their watches, radios and alarm clocks! I had to go up and point out to them that the students simply had to go and, reluctantly convinced, they grudgingly returned the articles, realising that the inevitable had to happen. It was moving to see them run out from the camp, following the cars of the departing students and weeping copiously. Some of the students also wept!

It was as a direct and totally unexpected result of this mission that soon after I received a letter which led me on to the next stage and introduced me directly to other folk currently working with Gypsies in Britain and, through them, to a remarkable movement whose existence up to that time I had never even suspected.

The letter was from one Fred R. Farr. It was dated 12 January 1978 and the letter heading, 'Gypsies for Christ', immediately caught my eye. 'We have recently heard of your work among Gypsy children,' the letter ran. 'A young member of our church was among the Oxford University team to visit you last summer. We are a young organisation seeking to offer encouragement and fellowship to all engaged in the difficult work of taking the gospel to Gypsies. We held a seminar at the Bulstrode World Evangelisation Crusade headquarters in the autumn when over thirty people joined us for the weekend. I enclose back copies of our magazine.' This was exciting! Here was encouragement, fellowship in the work, and the enclosed magazines revealed some of the work going on in scattered parts of the country among the Gypsy people. Clearly, as in my own experience, it was hard work but there were some results.

Of course I wrote back to Fred Farr and, from time to time, had letters from him and also from Bernard Mends, the secretary of 'Gypsies for Christ'. Then came a new development. In a letter in June that year Fred wrote: 'Remembering your request for a Gypsy evangelist, I have heard on the grapevine of a Gypsy church with a Gypsy pastor at Wembury near Plymouth. The man who can inform you on this is Pastor J. Fitzgerald of Plymouth.' That evening a gentle Irish voice answered my telephone call. 'Yes,' he confirmed, 'there is such a church at Wembury.' It was run by Jimmy and Doris Manley ('She has a remarkable preaching gift,' he told me), two Gypsies who had been converted through his ministry. Yes, of course I could come up and meet them; there was to be a Fellowship Meeting the following Wednesday and I would be very welcome.

We met that Wednesday evening and I followed him out to Wembury. The brightly-lit hall was owned by the church and the congregation, mainly composed of Gypsies, joined heartily in the worship led by Doris to piano-accordion accompaniment provided by Jimmy. When, later in the meeting, Doris preached it was quite evident that Pastor Fitzgerald had been absolutely right. With no background of study or training this Gypsy woman certainly had a real preaching gift.

Like most Pentecostal services there was variety. Another Gypsy woman, known affectionately to them all as 'Big Mary' sang, most effectively, some gospel songs she herself had composed; there was prayer of course, and I was invited to 'have a word'. Most memorable perhaps was the charismatic part of the service. There was speaking in tongues, some of which seemed harsh and not very pleasant but some of which had the beautiful quality that surely ought to characterise the exercise of the gift. When the pastor interpreted I wondered if his words were personally prophetic to me. 'Don't worry about your family,' he interpreted, 'they are in God's hands . . . a great harvest of souls awaits you . . . be entirely committed to God's purpose for you. . .'. Certainly the words spoke to my heart and I was, before long, to be privileged to see the 'great harvest of souls' in the Gypsy revival.

The meeting had started at half past seven and eventually Doris said, 'We'll close the meeting early tonight as our friend has to get back to Cornwall.' This was at ten o'clock! Pastor Fitzgerald and I were invited back to the Manleys' home for a 'cup of tea' which turned out to be a very good meal. We talked and talked, hearing the Manleys' testimonies which I was to hear given in public most memorably on two different occasions. They wanted me to go with them to France. In conversation it had emerged that I speak French and had some experience of evangelical work in that country. They knew that something very interesting in the way of religious revival was going on over there and they had heard that a great convention of evangelical Gypsies was to take place in Brittany the following August. Would I go with them? They would feed me and I could sleep in their caravan. I would dearly have loved to have been able to accept their offer but it was just not possible that year. But what was this convention? Who were these evangelical Gypsies? The vista of something much bigger than I had ever dreamed of was opening up.

What an evening it had been! I arrived home at about half past two in the morning, exhausted, excited and deeply impressed by the depth and vitality of their faith. Most exciting of all perhaps was this new thing: the fire I had just glimpsed.

Soon after this I had a letter from Bernard Mends, saying that he had just obtained the film *Ten Thousand Gypsies* and would be coming to Redruth in Cornwall to show it. He would also like to meet me and talk about the work. It was with considerable interest that I went to Redruth, accompanied by my daughter Heather who was doing a thesis on Gypsies for her college course, to meet him and see the film. It was a revelation.

It showed something of what was happening among Gypsies in Europe. Clearly there was a revival in progress and it whetted my appetite, preparing me for what I was later to see for myself.

Jimmy and Doris did attend the convention. It was at Ploudalmézeau in Brittany. They returned full of it. Hundreds of trailers, thousands of Gypsies, great meetings, mass baptisms all combined to provide them with an unforgettable experience. They had experienced some difficulty at first in finding the site of the convention. Big Mary, who, with her husband went with them, solved that. Having failed to get a Breton lady to understand her she simply shouted 'Hallelujah!' and the woman, smiling, knew where to direct them! Jimmy was most eloquent about the experience. 'There was a water baptism by the sea and there were thousands and thousands of Travellers, well, ten thousand of them all up on the rocks. I've never seen anything like it. There were so many people, and they stayed in the sea as the tide was coming up. It was marvellous, it opened my eyes because I hadn't really believed it, but I do now.'

Doris added her impressions. 'Oh, it was beautiful,' she enthused. 'I always used to think that people were making fun of the Travellers when they talked about their violins, because they don't play violins over here, but over in France they have an articulated lorry for the platform, the biggest platform you ever saw. They had flowers lining the front from one end to the other, and they were playing these violins.

'They had a dedication of babies and they asked for the oldest Gypsy preachers to come up and have the babies blessed and handed back to God, and do you know, the platform was lined with about forty Travellers that had been converted to Christ. They were preaching the gospel and were handing up the little babies to these dear men, to be handed back to God and to be prayed over. It was so lovely, and so different to be able to know that they loved the Lord Jesus Christ as their Saviour. There were some from Spain and some from Switzerland, but you could tell that they were really Romany Travellers, and all in love with Jesus. Little children were getting up, and singing. I have never heard singing like it in all my life. It was so well under control and it was really wonderful to see it . . . thousands of Travellers!'

This was something I really had to see for myself as soon as I could. I was now aware that some remarkable revival was going on but even then I was still unaware of its depth and extent. By now Bernard Mends had put me in touch with magazines of Gypsy work on the Continent and the outline was beginning to be filled in. I became increasingly aware that I was discovering a movement almost unknown in Britain, a great, deep movement of the Holy Spirit, and this moved me to the depths of my being. But still I had to continue with the nitty-gritty work of evangelism at the local level.

'When are the students coming again?' This was the recurring cry from the young Gypsies at Boscarne Park. The fact was that, despite the correspondence which the students faithfully maintained and occasional holiday visits, they were not likely to return. The team had inevitably split up on leaving college, some had married and they were scattered all over the country. Anyway it seemed to me that the time had come to try a different experiment in evangelism among the Gypsies. No one would be more likely to reach their hearts than Christians who were themselves of Gypsy blood. Jimmy and Doris Manley were the obvious ones and they had agreed to hold a mission in the area.

The date of the start of the mission was fixed for 29 April 1979, the second Sunday after Easter. We decided to try to obtain a marquee on the basis that the Gypsies might feel more inclined to attend a service in a marquee, and my church at Illogan Highway readily consented when I suggested the use of their premises.

Preparations were backed by prayer from many friends and I publicised the event as widely as I could throughout Cornwall and as far as Plymouth. For the opening service on the Sunday evening, those chapels in my section of the Camborne Circuit that usually held evening services agreed to close down and combine at Illogan Highway for the occasion and so we had a congregation of about 350. Forty or so of these were Gypsies from Boscarne Park. What to sing was a problem, not merely because of the limited number of hymn books, but also because most of the Gypsies could not read! I decided to break with the traditional form of service and use some sensible modern choruses including one for which I had written the words (some of which were Romany). The congregation sang it very well: '*Kushti Bokengro* (Good Shepherd), we will follow Thee', and we listened to the chapel choir singing 'Romany Chorus' on which Kenneth Pelmear, a well-known Cornish composer, and I had joined forces. The music and the words were intended to depict the hard, uncertain and nomadic life of the Gypsy folk and I tried to show that Jesus, nomadic in His own ministry with 'nowhere to lay His head', would be able to understand them.

I baptised some Gypsy babies and this led naturally to the introduction of Jimmy and Doris. The aim that evening was to introduce them and let people hear something about their background, their conversion and the great convention they had attended. The congregation was fascinated. Jimmy told of his birth in a tent and the stories of his youthful escapades and occasional brushes with authority amused the people, particularly the Gypsies who clearly identified with him and Doris. When he was talking of the bad temper he used to have one Gypsy woman shouted out, 'We're all like that!' Doris recounted how, as a younger woman, she had danced in a pool of beer and had been accused of petty crime she had not committed. The Gypsies nodded, murmured in agreement, they had experienced this sort of thing for themselves! Then she went on to tell of their early struggles as they started the Christian life, she spoke about their visit to the convention and, most poignantly and wonderfully, told how she found Christ. I can do no better than simply report her own words. As she told the story (and I have heard it again since) she held the congregation absolutely spellbound.

Doris explained how she had gone to church one Sunday evening, three weeks after the death of Jimmy's mother, a death made peaceful and painless following a prayer by Pastor Fitzgerald. 'After three weeks I still couldn't believe on Jesus Christ, and that night in the church when we bowed our heads in prayer I began to make up my mind I'd never come to church again. I thought, this isn't my life and I don't want anything to do with it. Then I began to cry, and looked up to see if anybody was looking, but everybody was in love with Jesus Christ. Then I put my hands together and I asked God if He was real, and, if Jesus Christ was real, to make me believe on Him. Suddenly, in the front of that church, there appeared a vision of the Lord Jesus Christ. I had never in my life seen a vision before. I have never seen anything like it. He was beautiful. He had these long white robes on Him, and long dark hair, and a little black beard, and a black moustache, but His face had rays of light coming from it, not like us. He was beautiful and He began walking towards me, and as He walked towards me I knew I wasn't fit to stand in His presence. I felt filthy and dirty, and as He came near He just touched me on the forehead. This vision went, and as He went I was begging Him to forgive me for being a sinner, and as I looked into the eyes of Jesus Christ I knew that, even though I was a Gypsy, thank God He loved me. So, it doesn't matter who you are, Jesus loves you.'

The people's appetite was now whetted and we announced the other meetings. The following day there would be the showing of the film *Ten Thousand Gypsies* and on the Tuesday the whole service was to be conducted by Jimmy and Doris. The first service had been an outstanding success.

Monday was not quite such a success. Many more Gypsies attended and there was a very good number present to see the film presented by Bernard Mends. Unfortunately, however, its message was really for adults so most of the younger Gypsies became bored and formed a continuous and rather noisy queue to the toilets! In fact the situation very nearly got out of hand and hasty arrangements had to be made to cater for the children in other rooms to enable the adults to see the film.

Tuesday was quite different. Again there was a large congregation. Again, there were quite a few Gypsies with a large proportion of children. Jimmy provided the music; Doris led the service. Some of us deliberately sat near the Gypsy children in case of problems and they did show some signs of unrest at the beginning. I was starting to get quite worried about what might happen when Doris started to preach. I need not have worried. From the very beginning she had their rapt attention. Deliberately and very effectively she identified herself with the Gypsies in her congregation. Old fashioned, very fundamentalist, her preaching got the message across and God spoke through her. When she'd finished she called for prayer and, to my utter astonishment, some of the Gypsy children were obviously engaged in their own way, hands together and eyes screwed tightly shut, in real and sincere prayer, rapt in the deep feeling of the occasion. People went forward for prayer and healing. I don't know what the results were in general as there were many people there unknown to me. What I do know for sure however is that a woman from one of my local chapels, though she did not go to the front, was permanently cured of a chronic migraine that she had suffered from for years and which had been getting worse.

Once again I had to face facts, inescapable facts, which knocked previously held views for six. I had frequently attacked certain charismatic practices (though I had prayed in tongues for years) on the basis that they were too often simply means of spiritual self-indulgence. Healing too, I had felt, was playing a disproportionately major role in recent Christian thought and worship. Yet here was healing that I could not doubt. Perhaps this helped to prepare me for what I was later to discover, the fact that the whole Gypsy revival had started as a result of an act of healing. I had to accept and adjust.

After visiting the local Gypsies, Jimmy and Doris

returned home and we all felt that, once again, a profound spiritual impression had been made and that local people were becoming more aware of the challenge of the Gypsies. It could hardly have been by chance that, only a week or so before, the Prince of Wales himself had visited the area and I had been invited to introduce him to some of the Gypsy boys. With pride they were wearing tee-shirts bearing the name of their five-a-side team 'Charlie's Angels'! The Prince was genuinely amused and chatted readily with the boys. This brought wide press and television coverage which, of course, helped to publicise the work. Soon there was to be more publicity for the next stage, a visit from some of the revivalists themselves, Gypsy preachers from France.

In January 1979 Bernard Mends had received a letter from France. Some Gypsy preachers in France wanted to spend time in England to help with the work among the Gypsies. They would come with their families, taking care of their own expenses. This was very interesting to me, of course, and when Bernard came down for the mission we discussed the possibility of them coming to Cornwall, and eventually invitations were issued.

On the morning of 27 May 1979 four Frenchmen turned up at my house. Only one, Christian Dufour, could speak English. He was not a Gypsy himself but was in charge of the Gypsy work in India where, I learnt to my surprise, there are millions of Gypsies. After only a few years of work there, he explained, there were now Indian Gypsy preachers, a Bible School and boarding schools for the children of that land, the cradle of the Gypsy race. Already something of the extent of this movement was beginning to dawn upon me. Another of the men, Tallis, was a real Gypsy, as were the other two. He had been a trapeze artist before his conversion. There was the big preacher, also previously with a circus, with the improbable name of Freddy; and Ramutcho, a Gypsy with a magnificent singing voice, as we were later to discover. We chatted over coffee and they then accompanied me to the morning service at one of my chapels. Christian introduced them and they sang, accompanied on the guitar by Ramutcho, who proved to be a very gifted natural musician. After the main service they took part in the communion service and their impact was such that one lady phoned me at lunchtime to say that the congregation that morning had been 'at the very gates of heaven'.

We visited the sites where two groups of Gypsies, real travelling Gypsies these, had recently settled for part of the summer. The four preachers overcame the immediate language barrier by using Romany words which were immediately understood by the English Gypsies. 'Yes, they're real Travellers,' said one excited English Gypsy to me, 'They know all the words.' I think it was then that my abiding interest in the Romany language was born. We squatted round a camp fire and the French Gypsy preachers were particularly keen to talk with the men. 'We must try to get the men,' Tallis kept on saying to me, and I began to sense the strongly male-orientated slant of the movement they represented. Giving an invitation to the Gypsies to attend the evening service at Illogan Highway, we left and returned to my home.

Lunch proved a lively meal! Theological discussion, polite argument, questions and answers enlivened the proceedings. It's surprising we had time to eat anything but the discussion was profoundly interesting. Here were youngish, utterly dedicated men, totally confident of the Spirit's leading, of little formal education (with the exception of Christian), who found aspects of English church life almost incomprehensible. More than one of them had been accepted into the French Gypsy Bible School before they could even read, and so the knowledge they had acquired of Biblical themes had gone into virgin ground and taken deep root. They were perhaps a little narrow-minded (I felt I caught more than a hint of Biblical legalism though this was probably due to their lack of wider, general education), but certainly they were single-minded. Infant baptism they just could not understand nor accept and they quizzed me closely on my view regarding the gifts of the Holy Spirit.

After lunch we visited the Boscarne Park Gypsy site where I had previously advertised the arrival of the French Gypsies. The local Gypsies were very interested and surrounded the French preachers, and I introduced them all round. I had the feeling they did not feel very much at home there, but of course we reminded the local Gypsies of the evening service and several of them promised to come. In the event, not one person from Boscarne Park attended that service even though I had arranged to baptise some of their children. Not one from Boscarne Park where I had been sweating blood for four years! I still don't know why. Happily though, some forty Gypsies came from the recently-arrived group we had visited before lunch.

I opened the service, performed some baptisms of Gypsy babies and then handed the meeting over to the French visitors. They were really impressive, their vitality and enthusiasm proving most refreshing. They sang, they testified (interpreted by Christian), and they preached.

Then I addressed myself to the Gypsies in the congregation. They had met and heard these real converted Gypsies. They had heard accounts of the great work going on among Gypsies in Europe. Did they want to follow Christ? I would, I told them, wait in the vestry of the church to see if any of them wished to talk to me. I brought no pressure to bear and, pronouncing The Benediction, went into the vestry where I waited a few moments in prayer. Then almost all of them came in! I feared that many of them had simply made a mistake, misunderstood me, and had come thinking they were going into the church hall for the promised tea and coffee to which the whole congregation had been invited. In about six or seven cases this was indeed the case and they were redirected. The rest stayed.

I talked to them straight. To follow Christ meant they were admitting their sinfulness and their need of Him, their acceptance of Him and their resolve to lead the Christian life. Yes, they all agreed, this was what they wanted. I was still not fully convinced though I wanted to be. One by one I asked them individually, by name, in front of their friends and families. Yes, this was what they wanted. I felt I should test it even further. I was going back, I told them, into the chapel which was now empty. If they really wanted Christ as their Saviour they should come in and kneel at the communion rail. They did, about fifteen of them. Large, tough, tattooed men, women with babies and teenage boys and girls knelt in silence. I asked the French Gypsy preachers to pray. This they did, at the same time laying their hands on the Gypsies' heads. They all prayed together, very loud, very fervently, partly in French and partly in tongues. The shock of this sudden, strange sound made some of the Gypsy girls giggle, but I believe this was simply a reaction of embarrassment.

Later we joined the others for coffee. The visiting preachers chatted as best they could with local folk and visitors from all over the area. Ramutcho sang again by popular request, he sang wonderfully. Too soon they had to go back to the Plymouth area where they had left their families in their trailers.

The following morning I visited the trailers of the local Gypsies who had responded. I cannot claim that they were soundly converted or anything like it, but the overall spiritual impression made upon them had been profound. 'What do you honestly feel about last night?' I asked one woman. 'I believed in Him before,' she replied, 'but now I believe in Him more.' One young lady who was leaving the area that day asked for a copy of the *New English Bible*. She was one of the few who could read and of course I was very happy to be able to supply her with the Bible she wanted.

Later in the day my wife and I travelled up to the site near Plymouth and, with Jimmy and Doris, visited the families of the French preachers. As we enjoyed their warm hospitality, there was more discussion, more information and more food for thought. Returning later to the site which housed the Gypsies who had responded in the service, I explained to them how the French Gypsy preachers travel around with groups of Gypsies, preaching to them and teaching their children to read. 'We wish we had someone who would do that for our children,' one mother observed wistfully. As a result of this, one of the chapel people from Illogan Highway performed just that service over a long period of time.

When we were saying farewell to the French preachers they said to me, 'See you at Ennordres'. I had now arranged, after various false starts and difficulties, to attend their forthcoming convention there, where I would undergo one of the most remarkable experiences of my life. At least now, before actually going to the convention, I had learnt what I had been trying to find out for several months. I had learnt how it all began.

TWO

How it all began

'There's no hope, you must face it, you're going to lose him!' The doctor was kindly, compassionate, but adamant. He had just operated on Zino the Gypsy; it was a case of tubercular peritonitis and there was nothing anyone could do. He looked at the young man's mother as he gave her the sad news. Typically Gypsy in appearance, her refusal to accept what he believed to be inevitable was equally typical. For Madame Duvil was of the Manouche tribe of the Romany race and the pride and passionate independence of her people shone in her eyes, was etched on her aquiline features. She had refused to accept the verdict of the woman healer she had at first consulted. 'There's nothing I can do,' the woman had told her gently. 'He has an intestinal complaint.' Zino's mother could not accept that; there must be some other person or institution that could help her son.

The hospital in the ancient Normandy town of Lisieux was always associated in her mind with the pious Saint Thérèse. Of course they would be able to do something for Zino, after all it was 1950 and these hospitals could do wonderful things. Her son was twenty years of age. Married, he already had a little daughter and his wife was expecting another baby. So to the hospital the family had taken him and had all waited, anxious, while the urgent operation took place. As the doctor had approached her after the operation she had immediately, instinctively seen in his expression the verdict she dreaded: 'no hope'. It couldn't be true and even if it were true she would not, could not, accept it.

So she howled. The poignant, age-old cry of the wounded Gypsy soul burst out, piercing, heart-rending in its intensity, swelling in volume, intensifying in emotion as her relatives added their not inconsiderable volume to this primeval plaint. The frenzied wailing shocked and upset the hospital. Vainly they tried to comfort the Gypsies, frantically they sought to quieten them, but it was useless. These people were disturbing staff and patients, their frenetic howling posing an unaccustomed problem with which the hospital could not cope. There was only one thing for it, they must be gently persuaded to leave the premises. But gentle persuasion did not work, the hospital staff becoming more and more impatient and frustrated, as the Gypsies refused to respond to their increasingly firm requests. Eventually, the Gypsies seemed to realise that little good would be served by remaining and left the building, still sobbing and wailing. At last Madame Duvil turned away and, with her in the lead, the sad Gypsy procession returned to their caravans, calmer now but mourning with a depth of sorrow all the more poignant.

Some months before, a Pentecostal pastor had handed Madame Duvil an evangelical tract as she was walking through the town. She had thought little of it and, at first, had thrown it down. Changing her mind she picked it up, put it in her handbag and forgot it. But God hadn't forgotten it! On the Sunday following the operation she had to do some shopping, and it was as she opened her handbag to pay the girl in the shop that she noticed the tract. Perhaps the girl would explain it to her? Helpfully the girl told her it was from an evangelical church not far away. She read out some of the activities advertised and one word shone like a ray of hope into the Gypsy's heart and mind: healing! That was all that Madame Duvil needed and, seizing the tract, she hurried out of the shop in the direction of the church.

The pastor was not to know that his service that day would be remarkable, in fact unforgettable. Not that Pentecostal preachers are unaccustomed to the remarkable workings of the Holy Spirit but this was to prove remarkable in other ways too! He was well embarked on his sermon and his congregation sat listening to the Biblical truths he was expounding. Crash! The door of the church flew open. The preacher stopped, the congregation turned round and were astonished to see a Gypsy woman, tract in hand, hurry excitedly, determinedly to the front of the church. Panting, out of breath, she wasted no time in gasping out her urgent request. 'My son is dying', she cried. Before the flustered preacher could respond she spoke again, pleading, peremptory. 'Come and pray for him,' she urged. The preacher regained his poise. This surely was of God. He spoke with the authority of a man inspired by the Holy Spirit. 'Your son will not die,' he assured her. 'God can do anything and He'll give him back to you.' The Gypsy was moved, comforted, convinced and the congregation thrilled as they recognised the unmistakable movement of the Spirit. 'Where is he?' the preacher enquired. 'We'll go and lay hands on him.'

Imagine the reaction of the hospital staff as the Gypsies returned! 'Lay hands on him?' The doctor was understandably sceptical but really nothing was to be gained by denying them their request; the boy would die anyway. He shrugged his shoulders and took them into the young man's room. Prayer was offered and hands laid upon the young man. No one could deny the sincerity of these people, and the hospital staff felt sad that it could do no good. Leaving a reasonable interval of time to elapse after the strange ceremony had taken place, the doctor carried out a routine examination of Zino. His fever had abated! With amazement that shaded almost into reverence he could not doubt that subsequent examinations showed him healed. The spark of grace that was to develop into a flame of Holy Ghost revival among the

Gypsies of the world had been struck in that room on that day!

Like the other great Gypsy tribes of Europe, the Gitans and the Roms, the Manouche tribe, descendants of early Gypsy immigrants to Europe, live nomadic lives, and the Duvil family was travelling at this particular time in the region of Normandy and Brittany. Madame Duvil knew that another son, Mandz, was somewhere in Finistèrre. Thrilled by what had happened, captured by the Christ whose power she now knew and gratefully recognised, she contacted Mandz and told him of his brother's miraculous healing. Mandz, receiving the letter, was puzzled. Something quite remarkable had clearly taken place but the whole thing had an unfamiliar, almost frightening ring about it. 'Come and see for yourself,' his mother had urged him. It was a 200 mile journey that faced him but one he knew he had to make.

Mandz made the journey and saw his brother, obviously now in good health and he heard the story, told in enthusiastic and picturesque detail, of the miraculous healing. He saw, too, a difference in his mother. Some new factor was influencing her, some new conviction gripping her, some new power was evident in her life. She maintained it was the Lord and persuaded Mandz to attend the meetings at the church to which she had run in such desperate need on that never-to-be-forgotten day. He was, perhaps despite himself, impressed. The evidence was there for him to see in his brother's healing and his mother's new, glowing Christian life and so the spark of grace was struck in his heart too. At these meetings he made the acquaintance of a pastor of the Assemblies of God, one Clément Le Cossec who, a non-Gypsy Breton himself, was destined to play a decisive role in the life of Mandz and the whole Gypsy revival.

Travellers, however, must travel and so the family eventually separated again and resumed their wanderings, this time with the real hope that the presence of

Christ can give. Mandz became a Christian and the life of faith developed within him. Two years later Mandz and his family were again in Brittany, at Brest. Christians always seek fellowship and it may be that they went especially to renew their acquaintance with Clément Le Cossec, the man they had met at Lisieux. Le Cossec was preaching in the hall of the Nouveau Théâtre when a group of swarthy Gypsies entered. Their wives were with them, long brightly-coloured frocks and headscarves proclaiming their Gypsy identity. Le Cossec, being the sort of man he was, almost certainly recognised Mandz among them and was able to adjust quickly to their presence. It may well be that he felt, as the congregation had felt at Lisieux two years before, the tingling thrill that comes when the Holy Spirit is in action. Different from his usual hearers though they were, he was deeply impressed by the intentness with which they drank in the words of the gospel it was his delight to proclaim. At the end of the service he went to greet them and now clearly recognised Mandz. After some conversation Mandz invited Le Cossec to visit them at their roadside encampment, an invitation which he was only too happy to accept. The following day he found them, their painted caravans forming a line along the hedges, with barefooted children playing on the grass and the dusty paths.

Invited to enter Mandz's caravan, Le Cossec and his friend from the Assemblies of God listened as Mandz opened his heart to them. He had an apparently insoluble problem. He and his wife, now, like him converted, had been studying the Bible. Their study of the New Testament in particular had convinced them that they should show their commitment and obedience to God by being baptised by immersion. Also, and increasingly, they were experiencing a longing to receive Holy Communion. Their problem was that, as was the case with very many Gypsies, they were not legally married although their commitment of love to one another was genuine, deep and lasting. Not being legally married, however, they were refused baptism by the pastors and, not having been baptised, were not able to receive Holy Communion. Le Cossec listened, saddened and shocked at the dilemma in which these sincere, simple Christian souls now found themselves, denied as they were the sacraments of the gospel. No doubt he could understand and to some extent sympathise with Mandz's feelings when he explained that, desperate now, they were on the point of baptising one another in the river! They were determined to obey God's commands, unorthodox though their method might be.

Moved and challenged by what he heard, Le Cossec determined he would arrange for a legal marriage to take place and invited them to the assembly's prayer meeting the following evening. The Duvil family were evidently sincere Christian people and Le Cossec felt that this was an important stage in their development. He was not to know though just how important it would prove in the event, nor that 1952 would see the Pentecost of the Gypsy revival. At that time, only a small group of believers, the assembly had no hall of their own. Evangelistic services were held in a municipal hall but Sunday worship and prayer meetings had to take place in the basement of the home of two members of the assembly. During the time of prayer one of the members, Louis Queinnec, received from God a prophecy announcing that there was to be a revival like a tidal wave. Naturally and immediately, the church people thought of their beloved Brittany but events later proved that it referred to the Gypsy revival.

Le Cossec was led by the Holy Spirit during the course of the meeting to devote some time for the reception of the baptism in the Holy Spirit. One can imagine his feelings when he saw that several Gypsies were kneeling to receive the imposition of hands for this purpose. Suddenly the Holy Spirit came upon one of them. It was Mandz! He was praying and praising God when suddenly he started to speak in other tongues as did the disciples in the Upper Room. So great was the power of God that he fell, head in hands, prostrate on the ground where he stayed for a long time, speaking loudly to start with, more calmly as time went on. As it was now getting late, Le Cossec gently lifted him up to his feet as he continued to speak in tongues in a low voice, his face shining with joy. It was almost as if, like St Paul, he was transported into the 'third heaven', not knowing whether he was in the body or out of it. From that day on everything was different with these Gypsies, for others experienced what Mandz had done; they were full of joy and their sadness at not being received into the communion service of the churches evaporated.

There came to the mind of Le Cossec the words of Peter at Caesarea, so relevant now to this situation, 'Can any man forbid water, that these should not be baptised?' and together they agreed on the day when the baptisms would take place, on the beach of St Marc on the outskirts of Brest.

Services of baptism are often very solemn, with each candidate clad in white, but the Gypsies all arrived for baptism clothed differently. The women had their coloured frocks, the men their trousers and coloured shirts, though some of them were stripped to the waist as they sang and praised God. Le Cossec, in fact, had a job to restrain them while they were in the water. At last they engaged in prayer and Le Cossec approached Mandz, baptising him in the water from which Mandz emerged joyful, hands in the air, thrilled to see the same thing happen to his family. Something new had happened, it had started and God alone knew what He would make of it. Now the Holy Communion. Again it was done simply, but how reverently! Deep emotions were experienced as they took the bread and the wine. For Mandz and his wife the moment had at last arrived for which they had so long and anxiously waited. The spectacular, thrilling blessing of their baptism was now followed by deeply-felt, profound joy and thanksgiving as once again they felt the Saviour's presence in his body and blood, a presence they were never to lose.

Time to move again though, so off they went, travelling once more in the inevitable, instinctive way of the Romanies, which is part of their very blood. As they moved, God moved with them. That this was a genuine work of the Holy Spirit was quickly evidenced by the fact that these Gypsy folk, thrilled with their new-found joy felt the authentic and automatic need to try to communicate their faith to others. Illiterate as most of them were, they could not communicate adequately in writing so they used the telephone! They telephoned their families and friends all over France. So it was that their kinfolk came from Bordeaux, Paris, Lille, Lourdes, Pau, Marseilles and so on, Gypsies in their scores under the impression that the gospel was only being preached in Brittany! Soon some of them too became converted and they, in their turn, went around just like the early Christians, testifying, spreading the flame.

Mandz and the others travelled, a line of caravans, the roads of Brittany. On one occasion, to the great surprise of the local population who watched, fascinated, through their windows, he hired a dance hall for their services. The gendarmes for the most part tended to keep them as far as possible from the local population, so they had to do unorthodox things like this. Then, growing more confident, they hired tents for their purposes and invited the locals in. 'Strange,' commented one villager, 'you don't see statues or a crucifix and yet you feel that God is there with them!' The Bretons, despite themselves, were deeply impressed by the ebullient joy and evident sincerity of the Gypsy Christians and one showed his appreciation by providing flowers on the table. This was in an area where previously they had been showered with stones! Now they split, going in different directions, some to the south for the grape harvest, others to the north, but all still witnessing sincerely, joyfully and very effectively. In Paris the news spread like wildfire and about 500 Gypsies attended the meetings as the prophesied tidal wave of revival swept along its invincible way.

To begin with it was confined mostly to Brittany, the territory in which the Gypsies most often travelled. They attended Pentecostal services whenever they had the opportunity but, despite the kind Christian fellowship they shared, it was not always easy for them to merge with congregations composed of people with a radically different life-style. In fact God had another plan. The Pentecostal Church, the womb from which they had been born, would see its Romany children grow in numbers and, whilst retaining the family likeness, develop in numbers and influence to form one of the most remarkable Christian bodies in the modern world.

So, in this, one of the most Catholic of the areas of France, the work of God among Gypsies was centred for about two years, from 1952 to 1954. Within the limits of this territory the flame spread slowly and steadily among the Gypsy population and the Christian gospel burned ever deeper marks into their character. The providence of God must surely have lavished special care and love upon this infant church.

The new Gypsy Christians felt the need of fellowship among themselves, and this of course was all part of God's plan, for part of the genius of this movement was to be its specifically Gypsy nature. In the past Gypsies who became converted were expected, encouraged even, to leave their normal, nomadic way of life and become absorbed in the sedentary life of the 'gorgio' (non-Gypsy). Now Gypsy Christians would stay with their families and tribes and would travel and, within that situation, develop as Christians. It would become an indigenous movement. Gypsy Christians would strengthen each other and win others of their own race to the faith. Usually, until numbers became too great, they would meet in their caravans, with increasing numbers outside the caravans. Passing folk might well have wondered to see, on occasions, groups of Gypsies standing in the pouring rain, oblivious of discomfort, as they listened avidly to the word of God.

In any lively movement problems, results of this very liveliness, are bound to arise. So it was that, in this embryo movement certain excesses and malpractices from time to time appeared. It was like the early Church all over again. The very intensity and spectacular nature of some of the spiritual gifts produced the sort of disorder to which Paul had to address himself in the church at Corinth. As at Corinth there were those who were slow to seek and find the 'more excellent way', that highest gift of the spirit, Christian love. This fruit of the Spirit and the sanctification of life of which it was an indication was not always evident and there was an unhealthy imbalance. When the quality of Christian love does not complement and refine the other gifts, things can get sadly out of proportion. Doctrinal errors also crept in. Certain Gypsies sought pardon at Holy Communion not only for sins committed during the previous week, but also for sins they anticipated they would commit in the following week and for which they desired pardon in advance!

Clashes between ancestral habits and the demands of gospel living also produced some strains as the nascent movement grew, although these were slowly resolved. Another source of trouble came from some priests who found themselves (not without some justification) perturbed at the growth of this strange movement. Some of them, to combat the revival, created new Gypsy pilgrimages, particularly at Lourdes, to distract the Gypsies from their evangelical conventions, which were soon to become so great a feature of the movement, and in some cases arranged to have Gypsies de-baptised!

Then there was the problem of leadership. Whose lead should they follow? Turning from the previously accepted authority of the priests, they found themselves seeking valid authority. Some Gypsies, ill-fitted and self-appointed, could thrust themselves into positions of leadership and exercise an authority which, unconfirmed by the judgment of their Christian fellows, could result in the shipwreck of their own faith and the confusion of the faithful, even to the scandal of the Gypsy church. Le Cossec knew that, as Paul had said in his letter to Timothy regarding the appointment of Christian leaders, they should not appoint 'a novice, lest, being lifted up with pride he fall into the condemnation of the devil'. He suggested that the biblical way would be to appoint elders. This the infant church accepted and it was a memorable and significant occasion when, after long and earnest prayer, a hundred men appointed four from among their number to be elders who would now oversee the work of God. Le Cossec gave them some basic training and it was with enthusiasm and humility that, under God, these men undertook their new and sacred responsibilities.

In 1958 Le Cossec felt convinced that God was placing upon him the burden of the Gypsy revival to an increasing extent. By now 3,000 Gypsies had come to Christ and they needed a shepherd. Growingly he felt God was calling him to give himself entirely to this work. What a challenge this presented! Three thousand new Christians with no church and, for him, no guaranteed income. No matter, it was the call of God and he accepted it, knowing as the years went by and the work grew out of all recognition that God had confirmed His call and led him into a work of apostolic scope.

Under Le Cossec's guidance the newly-appointed elders created independent congregations for the Gypsy Christians. Within five years the work had grown to such an extent in France that there were one hundred Gypsy preachers. At first they were sent on biblical courses at the colleges of the Assemblies of God. This however, did not always work. They were nomads by blood and to stay in one place, even a Bible College, for more than a short time was more than Gypsy flesh and blood could stand, so other arrangements had to be made. Again Le Cossec undertook this task of training preachers almost single-handed until a more permanent training centre for Gypsy peachers could be established.

Who would have thought, eight years before, what would be the results of Zino's healing? But this was only the beginning of the work, though this very beginning bears all the marks that make it unmistakably the work of God. If a board of evangelism had sat solemnly down and evaluated the possibilities of revival, would they ever have dreamed that it would start where it did? Church plans are normally geared to centres of population and certainly a Protestant initiative would have favoured the south of the country, where there had been so marked a Protestant tradition in the past. It is extremely unlikely that they would ever have thought in terms of strongly Catholic Brittany or Normandy. So, in an area totally unexpected and through the most humble of means, God commenced His work through the unknown man who gave Madame Duvil a tract. God was doing a 'new thing' among the Gypsies. But who, exactly, are the Gypsies, where have they come from and what have they suffered?

THREE

The Romany Trail

They are the other side of our nature. They are the free, independent, footloose people we would like to be, the seemingly uninhibited children of nature, unpolished by the false veneers of our civilisation. We envy them, love them or fear them as we become aware in them of the primeval depths we sometimes recognise in ourselves. They are the stuff of our fantasies, the readily available scapegoats on whom we project our own faults and failings. They are the inexplicable escapees from a troubled, misty past, the ultimate survivors in the fearful future.

The Gypsy 'king' was searching for his roots. We talked together, 'king' and 'rashai', about the past, the origins of the Gypsies, his people. I told him of various legends I had heard and mentioned the old story of the Gypsy who was forced to flee because he refused to make, for the Romans, the final nail to be used for the crucifixion of Jesus. 'No,' he said firmly. 'This is the one. They were about to put a nail in Him, here,' he suited the action to the word and struck me with his fist on the heart, 'but a Gypsy woman snatched it away.'

Who, then, are the Gypsies, where did they come from? Stereotypes about Gypsies abound. There are the romantic stereotypes: camp-fires, violins, simple, unspoilt children of nature. Then there are the other, sinister stereotypes: thieves, child-stealers, familiars of the occult and dispensers of poisons. Literature has unfortunately tended to perpetuate these stereotypes and an acquaintance of mine, Dennis Binns, an expert in Gypsy matters, has shown how this has happened in children's literature, as it also has in legend and rhyme.

My mother said
That I never should
Play with the Gypsies
In the wood;
If I did she would say,
Naughty girl to disobey.

Rhymes like that, popular folk-lore, fear, prejudice and false information have combined to form, in the minds of most people, a picture of Gypsies which lurches wildly and illogically from the sentimental to the horrific.

'Gypsies? From Egypt of course'; 'Romanies? I suppose we come from Rome': their origins are as mysterious as their nature. What is the truth then? We don't know for sure but research enables us to make some educated guesses.

The cradle of the race, says the consensus of opinion, is in the North West of India, the land bordering Pakistan, probably in the Indus valley. Nomadic tribesmen, they lived by travelling in the area, making and repairing metal utensils and, natural musicians that they were, by entertaining the folk with whom they stayed on their journeys. It seems that a large number of them may have spilled over into Persia following these pursuits. This nomadic, peaceful activity must have continued reasonably regularly for centuries among this low-caste, homogeneous group of tribes.

Then came a new factor. Here there is controversy, some maintaining it to be a fabrication of the Gypsies to gain acceptance in medieval Europe and others, including myself, thinking that it may well be historically true. The rise of the militant faith of Islam and the proselytising expeditions of Muslim Arabs into that part of India certainly radically affected the life of the Gypsy tribes. If, as some claim, and as seems very likely, they exerted militant, if not military, pressure upon the tribes to come under the banner of Allah it would seem to be sufficient reason for the wholesale movement of the tribes from that area. This, then, could have been their Exodus. So the Romany trail began. Slowly, irregularly, splitting into scattered groups, going in different directions they spilled over mostly in the direction of the west. Through the Middle East, the Near East, the Balkans they spread, fanning out in all directions on a trek that was to take the Romany people to Western Europe, Scandinavia and even the lands of the New World.

Their language sprang basically from the ancient mother tongue, Sanskrit. This was the root of the language, forming its main texture, grammar and character. As they travelled, however, staying for varying periods of time in countries through which they passed, they picked up 'loan words' from the languages of their hosts and absorbed them into their current speech. A comprehensive vocabulary of the Romany tongue will show this clearly. One I have in my possession characterises certain words by indicating their origin, Sanskrit, Bohairic, Rumanian, Bosnian, Turkish, Greek and so on. A German scholar once attempted to trace the journey of the Gypsies from the loan-words in their speech.

At last they came to Europe. Early in the fifteenth century the good folk of Arras in France were intrigued and perhaps a little frightened when a group of Gypsies arrived in their town. Black of hair and beard, the Gypsy men, accompanied by their womenfolk with their earrings and turban-style hats, claimed that the letter they produced was a 'reference' from the Emperor himself. (On other occasions the Pope was credited with writing it!) The fact that they claimed also to have come from Egypt gave rise of course to the name 'Gypsy'. As to names, the French name for them (apart from

Bohémien) is Tzigane, which is a straight corruption of the name Astiganes, by which they had previously been known in Byzantine days.

To start with, armed, as at Arras, with letters they claimed were from the highest authorities, they were generally, if guardedly accepted. Their very strangeness invested them with a mystery and magic they were in no way inclined to underplay and legends grew around them. Before long though, the increasing economic plight of European people tended to make them search for scapegoats and the Gypsies fitted the bill. Then it was that persecution started. They were hounded, whipped, hanged even, and country after country drove them from its frontiers. In Eastern Europe their status became virtual slavery so that, rebelling, many of them fled to Russia. In the fifteenth century they appeared in Greece and Cyprus, and the settlement of the main tribes assumed a roughly general pattern. The Roms (*Rom* is the Romany word for 'man') were found mostly in the Eastern European countries; the Manouche in Western Europe; the Cali ('black') or Gitans travelled mostly in Spain, Italy, Portugal and Southern France.

Still people had their legends about the Gypsies and their origins. They were descendants of Cain, priests of Isis or indeed, the ten lost tribes of Israel! So, for centuries they travelled, eventually reaching both North and South America. Usually they travelled in groups of varying numbers under their chieftains, some of whom were known as 'Captain', 'Count' or 'Duke'. The Exodus had taken place, the trek still continued for most of them. What lay before them was their equivalent of Calvary, which was to precede the resurrection and the great Pentecost, which would kindle a flame that would burn fiercely all along the ancient Gypsy trail even back as far as its origins in India, a religion that would offer the Gypsy race a new spirit, a new soul.

Some vestiges of the religion they had brought with

them from India still clung to their way of life and still influenced their behaviour. This animistic, Hindu-influenced religion was very deep-rooted and remained, and still remains, deep down in the hearts of many of them throughout their travels. Born survivors, they adapted, at least nominally to the religious beliefs and observances of the countries through which they passed and in which they sojourned for varying periods in the course of their trek. On arriving in Western Europe many of them, having been forced to become Muslims, now asked if they could be accepted into the Christian faith. That Christian faith took the prevailing hue of the area and they became Orthodox, Catholic or Protestant depending upon whether they were in Greece and Eastern Europe, the Catholic West or the Protestant areas of the continent. Some though, as in part of Yugoslavia, retained their Muslim identity. For them this was tantamount to retaining their Gypsy identity as acceptance of the Christian faith seemed to them to be a weakening of their Romany consciousness.

The old animism is still seen among many Gypsies in certain observances and taboos to do with sexual matters or hygiene and they keep staunchly to them even though they do not now understand their origin or their justification. A Gypsy girl once informed a group in which I was present that they never use the word 'rat'. To do so would inevitably bring bad luck in their business and other affairs. So, she continued, when they wish to name that particular rodent they use the word 'longtail'. This young Gypsy lady was well educated, participating, as I was, in a course on Gypsy education. What she did not apparently realise was that, in the Gypsy language, the word 'rat' means 'blood', about which there is a very strong taboo. So we have the admixture of ancient animism and some understanding of the Christian faith. The story about the Gypsy woman and the nails shows they knew something too of Calvary. Their own cross would leave marks upon the Gypsy psyche as indelible as the marks of the nails in the hands of Christ.

The personal cross for the Gypsies came with the advent of the crooked cross, the accursed swastika of the Nazis. The inevitable implication of Hitler's belief in the Nordic herrenvolk, the elite, the all-conquering Aryan whose very nature made him lord of the world, was that the untermenschen, the sub-humans, the Jews, the Slavs and the Gypsies were necessarily inferior, that they poisoned the holy stock and so must be exterminated. The stark fact, not generally known, is that between a quarter of a million and half a million Gypsies were killed under Hitler. He had them hunted out, he confiscated their money. If any of them were discovered, even if they had only one quarter Gypsy blood from a grandparent, he had them taken from home and work, even from his own armed forces, and put into concentration camps. As his evil empire extended he had special squads who sought out Gypsies in Poland and even in parts of Russia he had occupied. Anticipating his eventual conquest of Britain, he had note taken of Gypsy names so that, once master of that land also, he could carry out his work of extermination. 'From the Jews we do at least get some trade, but what can these parasites of Gypsies give us?' This was the philosophy, this the motive for the massacres.

In Buchenwald, Auschwitz and other centres of horror the Gypsies were herded, imprisoned and gassed in their thousands. Sometimes the Nazis used them, cynically, as guards for the rest of the camp and then savagely and suddenly rounded them up to go to the gas chambers with the very people they had been guarding. Someone noticed a significant difference between the reaction of the Jews and the Gypsies as they approached death. In the majority of cases the Jews went to their death with religious resignation. The Gypsies, born survivors (as, of course, were the Jews) fought tooth and nail to the very end. The Nazis too, differed often in their attitude to the Gypsies as opposed to the Jews. They rarely showed, in regard to the Gypsies, the same bitter hatred they had for the Jews. They merely exterminated them routinely because they were non-Aryan!

On arrival at the camps the Gypsies, men and women, had their heads shaved, their number tattooed on their left arm. Those who were too feeble to work were destined for immediate extermination. The fit were put to work and, in Auschwitz, as they went to work and returned from it they could hear the accompanying music of an orchestra, some members of which were German Gypsies.

Among the most articulate of modern Gypsies is Mateo Maximoff. Born in Barcelona of real Gypsy stock, he is a linguist, author and now a Gypsy preacher. He tells of 14,000 Gypsies being massacred in a single night at the camp of Auschwitz. Before the war from three to four million Gypsies lived in the Balkans, until the Nazis swept them away. Maximoff describes how, in the small Baltic state of Latvia, before the German occupation, five thousand Gypsies lived in peace after centuries of slavery. They succeeded in founding their own civilisation. Each family bought or rented a small house and a plot of ground. They worked in factories or in the fields, the children went to school and the young men pursued higher studies at college or university. Then came the war. 'They are only Gypsies like all the rest,' said the occupying power. So 2,000 were slaughtered immediately: forty per cent of the Gypsies of Latvia. About half of those who survived met with a terrible fate at Auschwitz. They included old men who were shot and then cast into those ovens that told no tales, children whose fate cannot be discovered and women sent to concentration camps to serve the pleasure of their jailers and then killed or sterilised when they were no longer required.

We could continue the appalling story of the genocide

of the Gypsies of Europe. What remains a glaring injustice is that, although the Jews have received some compensation for their sufferings, the Gypsies, as yet not effectively organised, have lost out on this matter. Efforts are still being made to give them their rights but it is not likely that they will ever be amply compensated. This obvious need for organisation, with especial reference to the compensation issue, has led to the formation of the World Romani Council. The Gypsy nation is beginning to acquire an identifiable body.

Perhaps the horror of the holocaust may have, in some profound way, helped to prepare the Romany nation for the discovery of its soul in the great revival. Certainly there are survivors, now committed Christians, who form a link between that horrific time and the new dawn of revival. Says Paprika, a Gypsy woman: 'On the way back from Auschwitz I weighed only seventy-five pounds and was very weak. I had caught a pulmonary congestion while I was in Béthune, in the northern part of France. Another Gypsy woman who had been with me in Auschwitz camp said to me, "If you knew the Lord He could bless you and heal you." I said to her, "I trust God, I pray to the saints." "No, it is not that, it's all new," she replied. "Now we can pray to the Lord for the sick and the Lord heals them. I can ask a minister of God to come if you want." I agreed and my husband went with her to see a pastor who came and laid his hands on me in the name of the Lord and I was healed.

'Then we learned that there was a mission with some Gypsies in Rennes, in Brittany. We went there with our trailer. There my husband and I accepted the word of God and gave ourselves to the Lord. Having lost all my family in Germany, who were burned in the cremation ovens, I had many dark ideas and nothing would satisfy me. The Lord has transformed me. I was baptised in water and now I am happy in my home.'

Her husband, Yayal, added, 'I have no father and mother, and no brothers or sisters. They all perished in the concentration camps in Germany. But I have found a new family, brothers and sisters in Christ in all the countries wherever I go.'

To this suffering people then, God came after the war. First the spark of grace in Lisieux, the slow development of the work over a matter of years and then another great advance as they discovered, and used to the full, the special method God had for them — the conventions!

FOUR

The Conventions

A number of years ago I was in a music shop in Plymouth where my young daughters were absorbed in choosing pop records. Browsing among second-hand 'oldies', I came across an old 45 disc which attracted me by the photo on the sleeve of some Gypsies and the French words '*gitanes évangélistes*' (Gypsy evangelists). I bought it and was fascinated to hear the fresh, fervent singing, especially of a chorus I had known from my time in the Salvation Army during the war. '*Un vêtement blanc*', its opening words, brought back a flood of memories. I knew its English version well:

A robe of white, a crown of gold,
A harp, a home, a mansion fair;
A victor's crown, a joy untold
Are mine when I get there.

Years were to pass before I realised that this was a recording of the singing at a convention at Rennes in France in 1958, featuring the American evangelist T. L. Osborn. When the French preachers had come to my home I told them about the record and later, in their caravan at Plymouth, Freddy's wife said to her husband, 'That's the convention at which your father was converted!' That, precisely, is what happened at the conventions.

It was a Pastor Nedelec, at that time working with Le

Cossec, whose idea of getting the Gypsy church together in conventions proved to be a stroke of God-given genius. So it was that the first convention was held in Rennes in 1954, a year of destiny for the progress of the work among the Gypsies. On that occasion 200 caravans were on site. For the convention in 1983 it was necessary to have a site twenty-five times the size of the first! Every year the numbers grew as it became a way of life for evangelical Gypsies to attend the conventions, and the attendant, though welcome, problems of organisation became ever more formidable. 2,000 caravans grouped around a large marquee is virtually a village of 10–15,000 people, bearing in mind that there are, on average, five children per family. Now the strategy is to have four conventions on the same dates instead of one huge convention. This really makes it easier effectively to minister to the spiritual needs of a growing movement like this.

From the small beginnings at Rennes in 1954 the conventions have grown, not only in size but in influence, and it is not uncommon to see civic dignitaries and even national leaders attending to welcome the Gypsies, or television cameras filming an event now recognised nationally as one of real significance. One feature of these conventions is that they not only bring together in fellowship those Gypsies who are Christian, but also bring in their non-converted friends and family members, many of whom have, through these means, come to a knowledge of Christ. Take Bob Ortica, born in a family of the Manouche tribe. His parents were not Christians and he, in his early days, had no interest in Christianity. He did, from time to time, attend meetings but was certainly not inclined to yield his life to Christ. Then, one day, he attended a convention near Paris where God used the preaching to bring him to conviction and so it was that he accepted Christ as his Saviour, a commitment which eventually led him to the Bible School to become a preacher.

The conventions are also used to inspire and encourage workers from abroad, working often in very difficult situations. It was a convention that helped to spur on the work in Finland, as a result of the inspiration received by a man called Mattaison, a Finnish friend of the Gypsies. This was at an early stage of the work in that land and of course not only did the work there receive encouragement, but the very presence of people like this contributed to the sense of joy experienced by the Gypsies at the progress and development of the work. Marquees were usually used although there was one occasion in Spain when they hired a cinema for their purposes.

The conventions also met a psychological need. Always on the move, the Gypsies felt the need from time to time to stop and meet with family and friends. This apart though, they met mainly to strengthen their faith, build themselves up in Christ and bring the unconverted members of their families to Him.

The work of organising the conventions is immense. A suitable site has first to be found, and this often takes a great deal of time because farmers and mayors are not always readily disposed to rent out their fields or their public squares. Once the site is found, however, the secretary of the mission writes to the prefect, the mayor and the chief of police and informs them of the place and date of the convention and its likely numbers. Notices are then printed and distributed to as many caravans as possible. Water services, toilet facilities, the collection of waste have all to be arranged. The great marquee, seating 10,000, has to be erected. Seats, floor coverings, a platform, electric fittings, loudspeakers have all to be installed. Food has to be made available, though the Gypsies normally cater for themselves. When the caravans arrive, in greater numbers every day, they have to be suitably sited. They are usually grouped in families and tribes, although they now mix more than they used to (evidence of the work of grace among the Gypsies). Even circus vans have been known to attend and lions have roared within the encampment! Once settled, tables and chairs, barbecues, washing utensils are taken out and set up, chickens run freely or are tied by the foot to the caravans, and if the dog is not too vicious it too is loosed!

The first night is the welcome meeting. Each morning there is a prayer-meeting at seven o'clock and at nine the preachers meet for prayer and Bible study. Three o'clock in the afternoon sees the evangelistic meeting and at five o'clock it is the turn of the young people in a smaller tent. The great dedication service will be at eight and at ten there is united prayer for the reception of the baptism in the Holy Spirit. So it goes on. Here Gypsy Christians are revived, instructed, inspired. Here those not as yet converted may well come into that experience. A convention is something to be experienced and I am immensely privileged to have done so.

I very nearly didn't get to the 1979 convention at all. I was unable to go with Jimmy and Doris the previous year but they felt sure that there would be another convention in 1979, and I knew that to attend it would be the next step in my growing understanding of the Gypsy revival. The assumption was that it would be at the same place, Ploudalmézeau in Brittany and at about the same time. It is not difficult to get to Brittany from Cornwall. You merely have the hour and a half's journey to Plymouth and then straight over to Roscoff by ferry. Of course, finance would be something of a problem, so I applied to the John Finch Travelling Bursary Fund of the Methodist Church. This was established to help ministers and students to gain knowledge and experience by travel. I outlined my plans and hopes for the convention and they kindly granted me £50. It would also, it seemed to me, be an opportunity for my wife and our two youngest children to accompany me for a holiday. So we booked the ferry over and arranged to stay on a camp site for the fortnight during which we understood the convention would take place.

Then I received a letter from Bernard Mends, who informed me that there would be no convention in Brittany in 1979! He had gone to a great deal of trouble to get definite information for me and this was it! He also mentioned that there was to be the first European Convention of Evangelical Gypsies in Central France that year, but that was to take place just prior to my holiday period and did not therefore seem viable for me. We were very disappointed of course, but decided, mostly for the children's sake, to stick to the original plan to go to Ploudalmézeau anyway, as the whole thing was already booked. We would camp, do it as economically as possible, and return the grant!

When Bernard came down for the mission, however, it transpired that he, with Peter Woolford, the half-Gypsy chairman of Gypsies for Christ, had arranged to go to the European Convention at a place called Ennordres by car. I could go with them if I wanted. I most certainly wanted!

Came the day, 23 July 1979. The convention was not due to start officially until the 26th, which was the date I would have to leave Ennordes to return home to Cornwall so that I could then proceed on to Brittany with the family! We were, however, assured that a lot would be going on and, in the event, this certainly proved to be so. Peter Woolford unfortunately could not come, but we were joined by Rev. Neville B. Cryer of the Bible Society (whose linguistic gifts and knowledge of the Continent were to prove invaluable), and Bernard's eldest daughter with her German friend.

Ennordres is in the Cher department of France between Aubigny and Bourges and that is a long drive down from Calais! We travelled overnight and arrived on a hot, sunny morning and made our way to the small château which housed the headquarters and the Bible School of the movement. The greetings were warm too!

The New Testament injunction to 'greet one another with a holy kiss' was literally observed and it was an unusual experience to be kissed on both cheeks by Gypsy preachers with garlic-flavoured moustaches! We were given a most welcome and refreshing breakfast under the awning of the trailer belonging to Jean Le Cossec (Clément's son), his American wife Nancy and their children. The bowls of steaming *café noir* and the French bread were most welcome.

At the first possible opportunity we strolled around the site. It was good to stretch our legs after the long and tiring journey and to escape from the crowds of young Gypsies who crowded round to gaze at our 'foreign' car. It was in very lovely wooded countryside (the area is famc for hunting and there had been strong opposition to the establishment of a Gypsy centre there) and all among the trees there were Gypsies. Gypsies standing queueing up at standpipes for water; Gypsies selecting live chickens from the travelling van for their evening meal; Gypsies preparing food; Gypsies eating in the open air; Gypsies plying their Romany trades of the curing of skins and metalcraft; Gypsies galore. The estimated number by the time we left was 15,000, the greatest number the movement had ever had at a convention, and it was still not officially opened! To walk around the camp was the experience of a lifetime. Gypsies of the three main tribes, the Manouche, the Roms and the Gitans were there, each with their distinctive dialect of the Romany language.

We saw Gypsy boys proudly demonstrating their prowess in gymnastic and acrobatic skills, doing back somersaults with ease and flair. Here were the brightly dressed Rom women, here the mischievous boys kept in order by men with canes who effectively and good-humouredly enforced discipline among the many hundreds of children gathered here. The majority of the trailers were gleaming, glittering and beautiful, the travelling homes of their proud owners. Some though were of the horse-drawn variety and their owners' way of life must have changed little over the centuries. In contrast to the more affluent who ate food cooked with Calor-gas, they cooked their food on wood fires in the open surrounded by dogs, chickens, ducks, goats, as well as their horses and a pony or two. The dogs, though there were hundreds of them, were normally chained up during the day but loosed at night. I didn't go out at night!

I met and talked with Gypsies from France, Spain, Belgium, Holland, Germany, Switzerland, Sweden, Portugal, Greece, Rumania, Italy and Argentina! Here again I met Tallis and Freddy, who was a sort of 'clerk of works' of the convention, and their families. 'Here is my brother,' said Tallis proudly, 'my brother in the flesh and now, praise God, my brother in Christ.'

We were well looked after. We ate with the other preachers in the dining-room and were found sleeping accommodation in an inn about ten miles away. On the night of our arrival we attended a great meeting in the vast marquee. Seating 5,000 people, it was full to overflowing, with people standing all round. A fourteen-piece Gypsy orchestra played as folk assembled and the meeting began a little behind schedule, Gypsies not being very bothered about time! With such a large crowd and with so many children (despite the men with canes) I suppose it was inevitable that the noise was loud and continuous and certainly that night it did not diminish very much.

There were choruses and hymns. I heard the familiar 'Vêtement Blanc', virtually their national evangelical anthem, and they sang a lovely catchy chorus (in French of course): 'When the Spirit lives in me, He makes me sing like David', before opening with prayer. This was quite amazing. When the leader of the meeting led in prayer it seemed that everybody in the marquee prayed out loud as well. As far as I could tell it was prayer offered rationally although perhaps there was an admixture of 'tongues', but certainly it evoked a most moving atmosphere of worship. When the leader stopped praying the whole congregation stopped too. Fervent it may have been but certainly, according to biblical advice, it was done 'decently and in order'.

Testimony was a keynote of the meeting and a German Gypsy woman recounting her healing from tuberculosis was quite typical. One problem that faced the organisers at this European convention was that of translation. It was partially solved later by the use of interpreters but this was not wholly satisfactory. One had to make provision for the variation of Gypsy dialects as well as the different European languages. We were very tired of course, but stayed on at the meeting until about ten o'clock. We noticed that, at least up to the time of our leaving, there was no Bible reading. This was strange for such a Bible-based church, but it probably had to do with the general state of illiteracy. One had to assume that their memory for Biblical passages was highly developed. I had previously noticed this in my contacts with the Frency Gypsy preachers who came to Cornwall.

Another thing I noticed was a fairly small hall quite near to the main centre. I thought its use was very significant and quite typical of the outlook and spirit of the movement. All day, every day, there was a continuous chain of prayer in progress there for the work, the convention in particular and the Gypsy mission in general. We had received a sort of programme, sent to all the presidents and delegates, which underlined the theme of the convention, 'The Action of the Holy Spirit,' and emphasised the main discussion point, which was how best to extend the evangelistic effort to the scattered Gypsy tribes all over Europe.

The previous day we had seen an open-air meeting of members of the Rom tribe, with songs and testimonies, miracles, healings, Spirit baptisms, the very stuff of Pentecostalism. Was not this the style of Christianity now making an important, if not major impact in the world? Was it not in fact (at least in some respects) the very Christianity of the New Testament itself? Before I left for this convention someone had asked me what I expected to see. My reply had been, 'New Testament Christianity', and the meeting of the presidents which I was to attend proved to be just that, although at the time I did not realise what a historic convention this would later prove to be.

The meeting of the presidents was under the chairmanship of Djimmy, president of the mission of the host country, France. Wisely, Clément Le Cossec did not take the chair but it seemed clear to me that the proposals put forward bore the mark of his own prayer, study and conviction. Evangelism was the priority, he explained. 'We must push evangelism, push it,' he repeated, suiting a gesture to the sentiment. The revival, he continued, was still growing. The work in Yugoslavia, for instance, was progressing well but now that people were thinking in terms of Europe, the tactics of the mission and, even more, its grand strategy, had to be adjusted.

Evangelism in the movement to date, he explained, had been carried out by and among Gypsies of each particular country. They all knew, of course, that the Gypsy race was divided into tribes. Would it not be better now to evanglise along tribal lines? Manouche could the more effectively reach Manouche, Rom influence Rom and Gitan win Gitan for Christ. There were, however, problems that would arise. For example it would not be right and fitting for Spanish Gitans to try to evangelise their tribesfolk in France without the courtesy of reference to the President of the French mission and without his agreement. The proposals, Le Cossec pointed out, were set out in detail in a paper that had been circulated. This paper outlined the areas of responsibility of national and group presidents, and attempted to establish procedures for evangelism, training, administration and financial matters.

The ensuing discussion was urgent, thoughtful, questioning and sometimes even a little heated. Patiently, Le Cossec went over all the points, explaining the reasons for his recommendations. The others did not always agree with him right away or completely, but such was the respect they had for this apostolic man that, at the end, agreement was reached. This meeting, as I later said to Le Cossec was like the Council of Jerusalem in the Acts of the Apostles.

This was indeed the New Testament church all over again, struggling, agonising with the problems of growth and facing the vexed, eternal question of authority. To have been permitted to attend it was a wonderful privilege and we were very grateful. The next step was for these matters to be discussed by the men of the three main tribes *en masse*, and then they were to be thrashed out in their 'workshops'. One can see here the enlightened leadership of this movement. There was firm, clear thinking and planning, yet a sensible desire to involve as many people as possible and win their agreement.

There were three meetings arranged now for the separate tribesmen (not the women!) to consider the proposals, but first there was a sort of briefing meeting in the marquee for everybody, where Le Cossec outlined some of his ideas. I will always remember him preaching on spiritual harvest. We were not, he told us, to be lazy or sleeping like some harvest workers described in the Bible. The harvest of souls was ripe and God was wanting us to work and give for the evangelisation of the world, for Jesus' coming would not long be delayed. If greatness in a preacher is the ability to communicate, then Le Cossec is a great preacher. Now calm and lucid, now humourously imitating the peculiarities of a tribe's speech or pretending to get in a temper like them, he could switch convincingly to the advocate pleading on his Lord's behalf.

When we broke up I chose to stay with the Manouche

because some at least of the talking would be in French. Bernard stayed with me whilst Neville went with the Gitans. Some of them apparently took a little convincing about the need for presidents. 'What do we need a president for?' one asked me, 'we have a president, Jesus!'

Leadership, then, was the main issue and certainly God has given leaders to this movement, great not only in numbers but in quality. One could see this as a result of the meeting of the presidents who are effectively leaders within their own countries and groups. Le Cossec himself, of course, certainly possesses the qualities needed by a leader of a movement of this nature. He has brains, initiative and the priceless gift of inspiring and training other people. Those now rising to positions of leadership within the movement also impressed me. For men, many of whom had not received the privilege of much formal education, their quality was remarkable. They showed dignity and a profound sense of responsibility without any obvious signs of conceit. Firm in their convictions they were, yet seriously ready to weigh up promising new ideas and suggestions. Another noticeable factor, of course, was their comparative youth. I have never seen any other religious movement with such a low average age among its leaders. Most of them would be in their late thirties or early forties, possessed of a native physical robustness which, allied to their evident spiritual power, made them effective leaders. They were all, of course, preachers and the flow of preachers into the work of the revival is yet another indication of its vitality.

Fairly typical was a young German Gypsy to whom I spoke. He had been baptised the previous year, he informed me, and hoped now to be a preacher. By the way he spoke and the conviction his words carried, it was clear this was not just a pious hope. Compared with the main-line churches of the West who are finding themselves hard put to maintain the numbers of their ministry, we see a great contrast in the Gypsy movement.

So many young men are wanting to enter the ministry that it is not possible to cater for them all.

So the leaders discussed the propositions, and reports were given by various preachers about the problems of their pioneer work. Bernard gave a report on the work in England and Tallis and Freddy spoke of their visit to us. Tallis told of a '*pasteur*' in England who gave them permission to preach in his church. 'It was hard for me to preach in a church,' he added. Then he pointed to where I was sitting. 'That *pasteur* is here,' he announced, 'stand up, *Pasteur*!' So I had to stand and received with some embarrassment the plaudits of the Manouche men, intended, I took it, not so much for me but for the work and workers in Britain.

A terrible thing had happened the previous day. An unconverted Gypsy had been out drinking and, returning, had fought with his wife and accidentally killed her. Just before we left the meeting there was a call for prayer for this man. He was heartbroken, we were told, he really loved his wife and was in deep need. We were asked to pray that God's forgiving and redeeming grace might come to him. I have never heard a crowd of men pray like that in my whole life. With one accord they rose to their feet, raised their arms and cried to God, begging, beseeching, like the old-time Christians 'pulling the blessing down'. I think God just had to answer that prayer!

Now we had to go, and although we were sad and would have liked to have stayed and shared more, I, for one, felt that so many impressions and experiences had come to me over those few days that I now needed time to sort them out.

My holiday in Brittany gave me the breathing-space I needed to assess what I had seen. It also gave me further insights into the movement. Walking along the dunes one day I came across a Gypsy family. Yes, they were Manouche and one had been baptised at Ennordres the previous year. 'He's a "Hallelujah",' explained his brother, 'baptised twice!' Knowing that the previous year's main convention had been in that area, I tried to find out the reactions of local people. 'Very interesting to see the baptisms,' was the general agreement, although one woman considered them 'a little light-hearted'. The local Roman Catholic priest though, recognised this 'light-heartedness' for what it really was. 'They have lots to teach us,' he observed to me, 'about joy and fervour.' His parish magazine spoke favourably about the convention too. 'Had their presence caused any problems for the police?' I enquired. 'Not at all,' the local gendarme assured me, 'except of course that an invasion of 10,000 people doubled our population for that period.'

I had now seen the church at work; Clément Le Cossec had chatted with me and given me an outline of the history of the movement and the place of the conventions. They certainly had played a vital and growing part in the growth of the movement, not only in France but elsewhere. Such was the growth in France that in 1978 the Gypsy church could claim that they had taken the gospel to almost all the Gypsies in France, that 17,000 of them were now converted and baptised, thousands were attending the meetings, 272 were preachers and that the church now had its own centre for administration and a Bible School as well as its massive marquee and forty-six places of worship for Gypsies who stopped travelling during the winter. For a church only constituted officially in 1957 this was growth indeed! It had been officially affiliated to the French Protestant Federation in 1974 and had become the spearhead of almost incredible missionary growth. This remarkable growth, from country to country, we will now try to follow, first of all into Western Europe.

FIVE

The Fire Spreads: Western Europe I

With the travelling habits of the Gypsies and the large families they tended to have, it is hardly surprising that the fire of revival spread, geographically, to other lands and down through the generations. Imagine the influence of one Gypsy woman converted at a convention at the age of seventy-nine. She had eight children, sixty-two grandchildren, one hundred and eighty-three great-grandchildren and forty-one great-great-grandchildren!

The fire spread to Spain, the Gypsy population of Spain to which George Borrow gave vivid life in his writings, Borrow was not to know the amazing things that would happen in that land in later years, yet one cannot but wonder whether his work played at least some small part in laying foundations for what was to come.

The Spanish Gypsy, known in Spain itself as Kalé ('black') belongs to the Gitan tribe of the Gypsy race. It was in the early part of the fifteenth century that these people first appeared in Spain, entering Barcelona in mid-century under their chiefs. By the end of the fifteenth century they had spread throughout Spain and today they number about 500,000 in that land, with about another 50,000 in neighbouring Portugal. Some moved over into France later and some emigrated to South America. Although they do not now generally use the ancient Romany language, they still retain some of its words which they use in the course of normal conversation whilst speaking the Spanish language. They dress very similarly to the Roms, with whom they feel a strong sense of closeness, but have little natural love for the Gypsies of the Manouche tribe, an antipathy happily forgotten as folk of both tribes come to the experience of the living Christ. (One of the great sights of the conventions is to see the tribes mingling as never before, thus testifying to their new-found unity in Christ).

Like most Gypsies, deeply involved with their extended families, they tend to lengthen and intensify the period of mourning when one has died. At such times they would normally refuse even to play the guitar, although now the new understanding of the Christian gospel with its hope of resurrection and heaven has done something to change this. In some meetings now, even when mourning is still being observed, they will often accompany the singing on the guitar. Music is, of course, a great feature of their life and Gypsies singing, playing and dancing to flamenco music are a well-known feature of Spanish life.

It was with a pastor by the name of Rodriguez from Barcelona that the revivalists first made contact. This man had discovered a strange and very needy group of Gypsies. It would be fascinating to know just how he discovered them and precisely how he contacted them and learnt their story. He must have heard that Gypsies of another tribe, although with resemblances to the Spanish Gitans, were living in wretched conditions in tumble-down shacks in his area. As this faithful minister made, or tried to make, some initial contact he must have found communication very difficult, for these were Roms who had migrated from Yugoslavia. Why they moved to Spain we can only conjecture. What however was certain was that they were a lonely and neglected minority. So he visited them in their pathetic shacks. He overcame the problem of communication. Slowly he established a link with them, gradually gaining their confidence, and then he took the gospel to them. Here was down-to-earth, hard evangelistic effort to which God added His blessing because Rodriguez, to his joy, saw some of them come to a knowledge of Christ. He had heard of the growing revival among Gypsies in France and he persuaded some of his Rom converts to go with him to the convention at Toulouse in 1957. This proved to be a very fruitful contact; the Roms from Spain were helped and strengthened and the French Gypsies encouraged to see that God was working in other lands.

It was as a result of this initial contact that, in December 1961, Clément Le Cossec launched a determined effort to win Spanish Gypsies for Christ. With a team of Frency Gypsy preachers, his first aim was the evangelisation of Gypsies in Barcelona, and here it was that the local knowledge of Pastor Rodriguez proved invaluable. One of the results of this work was that the following year some of these Spanish Gitan Gypsies were able to attend the first gathering of Christian Gitans in France, thus gaining new insights, making new friends and renewing their mutual faith.

Alongside this purposive, organised evangelism there was an example of 'gossiping the gospel', the very natural and spontaneous spread of the revival in a completely different and very authentic way. Some Spanish Gitan Gypsies were travelling in France, where they met some other Gitans. These were Gitans who had been converted in the revival and who were eager to witness to their new-found faith. As the Spanish Gitans listened, there were among them two brothers to whom this witness came as a clear word from God. The two brothers were converted and, returning to their own land in 1967, they in their turn witnessed to Christ among their own folk. In the work of the spreading of the gospel nothing is more potent than the simple, convincing testimony of someone into whose life the Holy Spirit has come. The witness of the brothers was not only very effective but significant. Unplanned, spontaneous, it broke new ground in Spain, for now Spanish Gitan was testifying to Spanish Gitan. It was working along tribal lines (anticipating the strategy suggested at the Ennordres convention), across national boundaries as the work of the gospel spread.

Later the brothers were joined by other preachers and all of them had to face great difficulties for there was no real religious liberty in Spain. At any moment they could face arrest and imprisonment and some of them did. On one occasion it was whilst some were actually in the process of preaching that they were arrested, imprisoned for ten days and only freed after the intervention of a high official. It was not until 1971 that the Gypsy mission, officially recognised now under the name of '*Filadelfia*' obtained religious freedom. This meant they were now able to gather more than twenty people together without prior permission. This new freedom certainly helped with the growth of the revival and in Madrid, for example, a flourishing church grew up under the care of several elders, more than a thousand Gitans were reached with the gospel and preachers began to appear from their own people.

Felix Ritz, a young pioneer preacher of those early days, first visited Spain in 1962 and took part in a missionary tour in 1965. Under the existing conditions there was nowhere for them to meet. A Christian lent his house (later to become the national centre of the Spanish Gypsy Mission) and there were many occasions when they had to meet in garages or barns. It was not, though, until 1967 when he accompanied another great pioneer, Emiliano, that he saw the start of the Spanish Gypsy revival in a very real way at Valladolid. The meetings took place in the wooden shack of a Gitan and this was to be the meeting place of the Gypsy church for some years, until the local Christian Gitans were able to acquire a suitable centre. When they did, it became the meeting-place, week after week, of 400 or so Gitans who would meet to praise God. Even when persecution passed, the government looked with disfavour on the word 'movement' or even 'Gitan', and so they adopted the name '*Filadelfia*' (brotherly love) to avoid problems. In the days of General Franco they had been forced to carry out their baptisms in isolated places. Meetings with over eleven people had not been permitted, nor were meetings in tents, but at last they had a centre of their own.

It was, in fact, in January 1966 that the first eight Spanish Gitans were converted in the north of Spain, and it is some indication of the growth of the movement in Spain that ten years later about 8,000 Gitans were baptised, sixty-eight churches were in being and some 320 Gitan preachers were active! The movement was particularly fruitful among young Gitans, and in 1976 it could be claimed that more than a hundred young Gitans were deeply motivated by a vocation for the work of Christ. So there was a need to prepare them, and this need was wonderfully met when a couple of non-Gypsy Christians, led to Christ by the Gypsy church of Salamanca, made the generous gift of a fine piece of land upon which a Bible College could be built. At this time too, a Spanish Gypsy, the preacher Pako, was studying hard to prepare himself to take the gospel to his fellow Gitans of Argentina. Spain was now sending out her own missionary!

So this country proved a very fruitful ground for the revival and the church grew. In 1972 the work was divided into three large regions, each under the care of a preacher, and together these three constituted the council directing the movement nationally. The American Pentecostalist, T. L. Osborn had, as we have seen, been involved in an early convention and his organisation had given money for this work in Spain, as had some Norwegian Christians. So, with this help, the mission was able to report that thirty-eight places of worship had been opened in three years. In Madrid alone, ten places of worship were opened in one year, attended by about a thousand Gitans, whilst in one city 300 Gitans were won for Christ after the opening of a new hall. Opposition, though, had not quite died out, for in 1977 a Gypsy preacher was sentenced to six months in prison by the Catholic tribunal of Granada for having 'publicly burnt pious images and idols'. The zeal of this good man may perhaps be queried by some and one can understand the reaction of the authorities, but it has to be realised that Gypsy Christians wanted to disassociate themselves from things they now regarded as superstitious and which, with a lively personal faith, meant nothing to them.

By 1979 more young men (no female Gypsy preachers here!) were hearing the call to preach and the need for a training centre to be built to prepare these men for a preaching ministry was becoming more and more urgent as the church grew and needed them. There was hope that some such centre might be created near Madrid and this surely must have been one of the burdens of the prayers of the Gitans preachers as they came together in the February of that year. No doubt they gave thanks for the publication, distributed free, of a Gitan Christian review in Spanish *La Luz del Mundo* (the light of the world).

The pastor, Palko, responsible for the administration of the work on a national basis, told them of a Gitan church in Madrid. Its name is '*Pan Bendito*' (Blessed Bread), and it is one of over a hundred such throughout Spain with its own Gitan pastor and with meetings every night of the week. A vibrant community, it grows continually and boasts a large number of young people who not only study the Bible but preach the gospel in their quarter of the city, and who are totally committed to the concept of the proposed Bible School.

It was about this time that a remarkable thing was reported by the Gitan pastor at Coruna, Ramon Salazar. Whilst he was taking a meeting his young daughter fell from the balcony of their home and was rushed to hospital. Like Madame Duvil at the beginning of the revival, he and his wife rushed to the hospital and anxiously sought out their daughter who, to their astonishment and to the astonishment of the doctors, seemed to have escaped harm! She had been X-rayed but there was no fracture, no wound! The child then asked to go to their meeting and, as they made their grateful way there, her father asked her what she remembered of falling to the ground. Imagine his surprise when she told him she had not fallen to the ground but into a river! His already firm belief in angels was reinforced when the child told him that, in the river, there was a little boy with her dressed in white!

Later in 1979 a group of Spanish Gitans attended a convention in France (the Ennordres convention which I attended) and thought was given to the advisability of closer co-operation between those working in Portugal and those working in Spain for now, it was announced, there were almost 500 Spanish Gitan preachers at work in Spain, France and Portugal. The year also saw a national convention of Spanish Gitan preachers which took place in a cinema in Madrid. Over 300 preachers were able to attend, most of them young men of between twenty and forty years of age. The past President, Jaimé, one of the two original brothers converted in the early days, was now going to concentrate on the work among Gitans in Barcelona and was to be succeeded by a preacher called Péllélé, whilst Palko was confirmed in his work of national administration.

In 1981 the preacher Gimenez Manico found himself responsible for the task of unifying the efforts of evangelising Gitans throughout the world. This, of course, was to implement the agreed Ennordres strategy of evanglising along tribal lines. He attributed the success and rapid growth of the work in Spain to the decision of the Holy Spirit to prepare workers and to send them out into the world. Certainly this missionary effort, emanating from Spain, was a signal proof of the Spirit's activity as the work spread among Gitan Gypsies who travelled to South America.

Still there was growth within Spain. The national convention of November 1982 noted that, at that time in Spain, the number of preachers, including candidates to the ministry now numbered 700 and that at Balaguer there had been a revival among the '*payos*' (non Gypsies). Thirty had been converted and had joined the church. Here we see what was to happen not infrequently during the revival, the convincing witness of Gypsies winning to Christ those outside the Gypsy race. And the growth of preachers! The now established Bible School on the outskirts of Madrid would be well used.

1983 was hailed by Miguel, a French Gitan preacher, as seeing a new breath of the Spirit passing over Spain. It was now influencing musical circles and four artistes had been converted. One, Pedro Poubil, known throughout Spain and the Spanish-speaking world, had come to Christ in 1982. Film actor and recording star, he had placed his ranch at the disposal of the Gypsy mission for meetings. Now, breaking totally with his past, he had resolved to sing and play his guitar solely for the Lord. From the same sort of world came 'La Chana'. A dancer from her youth, she became one of the best exponents of the flamenco dance in Spain, but refused a tempting offer to dance on television soon after her conversion. Her husband, whose father was also a Gypsy, supported her and declared that now they belonged to Christ and would not play the guitar and dance for worldly reasons.

Clément Le Cossec himself, reporting in 1983 from Madrid, tells of twenty Gypsy churches in various parts of the city. The centre where he spoke was full to overflowing and many had to stay out of doors. Now there were more than 850 preachers! Now the Gitans were evangelising the non-Gypsies for one preacher had told him that eighty per cent of his members were '*payos*' whom the Gypsies had won for Christ! A Valladolid they were planning the construction of a great evangelistic centre with places for 3,000 people and in that place alone there were forty preachers. By 1984 30,000 Gitans were baptised and 1,000 preachers were caring for them! But what of Spain's neighbour, Portugal?

Gomes Lopes, a Portuguese preacher, lay seriously ill in 1958, totally unaware that through this illness God was to lead him to work among the Gypsies in his land, Gitans like those of Spain. He was suffering from a serious lung disease and had prayed continuously and desperately to be healed. On one occasion whilst he was praying he had visions – visions of Portugal and its Gypsy people. He clearly heard a voice which said that no one took the gospel to the Gypsies and that he should go to them because the Lord wanted to save them. How could this be? he wondered, when it seemed that his life might even then be approaching its end. The voice came again: the Lord would heal him so that he would then be able to go to the Gypsy folk of his land.

The healing took place, although it was not for over a month that it was complete and he had the clear conviction that it had been conditional upon his willingness to go to the Gypsy people. He was at that time an evangelist in connection with the Methodist Church and he was also a professional man. Committed as he had been to this way of life, it is not surprising that for two years he held back, wondering in fact whether or not it had all been a dream. One day he found himself near a Gypsy camp. He had the uneasy feeling that the Lord had led him there and, astonished to see so many Gypsies, it seemed that the Lord was reminding him of His command. Deeply moved, moved indeed to tears, he sought the Lord's pardon for not having obeyed Him thus far.

One can only guess at the reaction of his wife when Lopes suggested, a week or so later, that they should go and camp with the Gypsies but, good Christian soul that she was, she agreed and went with him! It is, to say the least, very rare for non-Gypsies to do such a thing and the Gypsies were curious, perhaps not a little suspicious. When they asked him what he was doing amongst them, what he was trying to say, he simply told them that he wanted to speak to them about Jesus. So he spoke and many of them gave him a courteous hearing, so much so that when he asked if he might return at a later date, they readily agreed.

The news spread among the Gitans and the invitations to him to speak to them increased. When at last he was invited in 1962 to go to Lisbon, the capital, to speak to the Gitans there, he felt that the vision had been vindicated, a conviction strengthened when, six months later, Clément Le Cossec with his apostolic band of Gitan preachers visited Portugal. Ten years later Gomes Lopes was still in charge of the work, now supported financially by the Swiss Protestant Gypsy mission. The parent movement, having discussed the work in Portugal at a retreat in Madrid, took the decision to send valuable aid in the shape of Spanish Gitan preachers, three men who volunteered to work, with their families, in Portugal. This work was concentrated mostly in the south of the country where they worked closely with Lopes among the poverty-stricken Gypsies of this region.

1977 found the Spanish preacher, Emiliano (one of the two Spanish Gypsy brothers converted whilst travelling in France and, ever since in a position of leadership in the work among the Gitans) working in Lisbon. He could report with joy a time of miracles, transformation of lives and the defeat of evil forces. Moreover, he had conducted fifty-five baptisms! A church had been opened and the whole of the cost had been borne by the new converts. The following year Clément Le Cossec gave further impetus to the work with his intrepid team of French evangelists.

The nascent revival, though, was being hindered by the lack of native Gypsy Portuguese preachers. It was not until some years after Emiliano and his brother Manolo, also a preacher now, came to help that the revival was renewed and Portuguese Gypsy preachers emerged. In 1978 there were ten of them but numbers were clearly on the increase and they were badly needed not only for the continuing work of evangelisation, but to care for the growing number of Portuguese Gypsy converts who now numbered some 500!

Conventions, as in other countries, were now beginning to be held and the third was held near the city of Faro in August of 1979. Visiting it, Clément Le Cossec was struck first of all by the evident spiritual progress made by the preachers, their bubbling enthusiasm and their keen wish to extend their evangelistic mission to all the Gypsies in their land. A sign of the health of this group was that two new preachers were consecrated to the work of the ministry after three years of training and testing. He was also pleasantly surprised by the presence of non-Gypsy Portuguese folk, equally zealous, mingling with the Gypsies. Near Fano, where the convention took place, the Gypsies, under the guidance of their Gypsy preacher, had built a new centre capable of seating 300 people. About 200 already attended regularly and, surprisingly, only fifty of these were Gypsies, the rest non-Gypsy Portuguese. The missionary work of the Gypsy mission in Portugal was now under the direction of the Spanish Gypsies Emiliano and Manolo, helped by several Portuguese Gitan preachers and co-ordinated by the preacher Palko.

Here again we see the native vitality of this movement, moving now with increasing success not only to other countries but to people outside Gypsy life. At this convention there sat a 75-year-old Gitan man, his face radiant with joy. Father of twenty children and grandfather of two hundred (he'd lost count of his great-grandchildren!) he glowed with happiness to see one of his sons consecrated to the service of the gospel. This convention must have been a sight as Gitans came with their donkeys and mules and camped in tents around the marquee! For some of them were poor and, though giving priority to the preaching of the gospel, the movement rightly tried to make provision for their poor, supplying them with necessities, especially clothing. A great welcome was given to the President of the Evangelical Alliance as he came offering help from the Portuguese Protestant churches because it was now recognised that the fastest growing work among the churches in the country was that of the Gypsies.

At a later convention near Lisbon, late in 1981, it was observed that the work still progressed slowly (though what was 'slowly' for these people might well have been considered quite remarkable progress in other churches!) Preachers were still few and poverty remained widespread so Emiliano appealed for help to supply the material needs of the people. Still the work of evangelisation proceeded though, and the faithful preachers travelled far and wide in Portugal proclaiming the gospel to the scattered tribes of Gitans.

Over now into Italy, where some hundred thousand Gypsies live. That this would prove a difficult country for the Gypsy mission there could have been no doubt. Strongly Catholic in some areas, passionately communist in others, there would clearly be great obstacles to overcome. For over twenty years, commencing in 1963, efforts had been made to reach the Gypsy population of this land, to touch the two main tribes, the Sinti (another name for the Manouche) and the Roms. Some courageous preachers went down into the south, even as far as Calabria and into Sicily to conduct missions, whilst others went to the north on the same errand, but the results had been minimal.

In 1972 only two preachers were left working in the country and the Gypsy mission as a whole was presented with an urgent appeal to support the cause in Italy with prayer. By 1978 there was little real improvement and the mission had sadly to report that their efforts over more than twenty years had achieved little and left them very discouraged. The first contacts with the Sintis had been faithfully made but, just as it seemed that the revival was about to take off, there was a strong reaction from the Catholic Church. Despite this, however, some families had been won for Christ and that was a cause of real rejoicing. A further tentative effort was made by two visiting preachers but they were unable to found a lasting work, this time because of financial strictures. Further attempts were again made and more failure was experienced. The picture was grim.

Then came 1977 and another new initiative, this time by two French preachers. As a result of this a revival started among a group of Roms who had come, via France, from Bulgaria to settle in Italy. Following this an Italian, Paolo, now agreed to work full time to help the preacher Fardy who had come from Sweden and, with Yacob, a preacher who had previously worked in the country, they made a determined evangelistic 'push'. Clearly the work among the Roms had at last really taken off and here there was evidence of the sort of thing that had characterised the work in France and Spain. In about a fortnight around seventy were baptised in the Holy Spirit and about one hundred baptised by immersion. In addition to this, men were beginning to come forward to offer for the ministry.

By 1980 it was reported that this revival among the Roms was making constant progress, new baptisms bringing the number of converts to more than 120. There were now three Italian Gypsy preachers caring for the small flock and launching new evangelistic efforts with the aid of visiting preachers. That year missions took place in a new marquee in the region of Venice, and at Rome, where about 500 caravans assembled for the people to hear the word of God and pray.

The church at Milan was well established in 1983 and led by two Italian Gypsy preachers. The year 1983 was in fact a decisive year. A mission held in June of that year was as a result of an urgent and pressing request of some Italian Gypsy preachers who believed the time was ripe. To start with it seemed unpromising. There were only a hundred or so caravans and the spiritual life of those attending was very low. Certain other difficulties that arose brought a great deal of discouragement and morale became extremely low.

Then the Spirit moved and revitalised the whole thing. Imagine that marquee and picture some fifty men standing up and expressing repentance, with a firm vow that henceforth they would commit their lives to the faithful following of Christ and consecration to His service! Gypsy women admitted that they had often told fortunes and now promised, with the Lord's help, to do so no more. (The clear need to abandon such activities, so much part of the normal Gypsy life, posed great economic problems to many Gypsies. Some were told, like Jimmy and Doris, that they would starve if they became Christians. One Gypsy told me that he knew of some in America who had given up their faith because they were now unable to feed their children.) Another significant thing took place at this gathering. It was decided to seek the help of the Assemblies of God, and a meeting was arranged between the leaders of the mission and the leaders of the Assemblies as a result of which the Gypsy mission was welcomed into the Assemblies' fold whilst being assured of their continued autonomy.

In the following September, a great convention was held at Milan and the truly international character of the movement was clearly demonstrated when Gypsies arrived in caravans from Sweden, Germany and France. So, in unity together, they affirmed their solidarity in Christ, a solidarity in addition to the linguistic unity that prevailed, for all of them, including the Italians, spoke the same Romany language. With this solidarity as a background, they decided to increase their efforts to reach the Sinti tribes. It was in the great marquee, brought especially from France for this purpose and surrounded by more than 400 caravans, that this great consultation took place. Everyone was asked to make some new missionary effort to help the work and to pray with fervour for the Spirit of God to touch the hearts that were to hear the Word as a result of this new dimension of mission. So it was that the revival in Italy came of age.

René Zanellato and his wife Filia (a Manouche Gypsy) had about 1,000 kilometres still to travel. Commissioned by the Gypsy Church, they were to make a special missionary journey to the Gypsies in Greece. As he approached their van, René failed to notice the patch of oil on the surface of the car park. He slipped on it, fell heavily on his right elbow and broke it, badly. To most people this would have signalled the end of their mission, at least for the time being. But these folk are made of sterner stuff. They talked it over, got medical first-aid treatment and, deciding the event was the work of the Devil, who clearly did not want them to go to Greece, they decided to carry on. And so, for 1,000 kilometres they travelled, René turning the steering wheel with his left hand, whilst Filia manipulated the gears!

The Apostle Paul, one time evangelist to Greece himself, would surely have approved of the Christian dedication and determination of this couple committed to taking the gospel to the Gypsies of that land. For there are some 500,000 Gypsies in Greece, five times as many as in France. The Djambazi tribe, nominally Orthodox in belief, knew nothing of the work of God; they were to hear of it for the first time as a result of the revival and the efforts of missionaries like Zanellato. An interesting fact is that they bear a marked resemblance, both in appearance and in language, to the Manouche of France. This of course would be of immense help to René and his Manouche wife.

Some Gypsies had come to Greece from Rumania by way of Yugoslavia. Having been slaves in Rumania in the seventeenth and eighteenth centuries, they had been forbidden to use their native Romany language and so only a few words of it remained, interspersed within the Rumanian language they normally employed. It is interesting too to note that a surprisingly large number of Greek words have entered the Romany tongue as, in their trek from India, the Gypsies borrowed words from the lands in which they stayed for any length of time.

It was at Alexandria in 1971 that René, with other missionaries, had first commenced his work amid the Djambazis. Some miraculous cures were recorded and certainly a valuable contact was made. The Gypsy musicians, a feature of Greek life, showed interest in the meetings which were held for them, and they were all able to understand what was going on, for the conversation was in Rumanian, Yugoslav and Romany. Several families of the musician Gypsies lived near Thessalonica and it was discovered that a number of Roms were closely engaged in commerce in that area, and so it was to Thessalonica and its outskirts that the eyes of the missionaries turned. At about the same time a small community of Manouche Gypsies was discovered in the area of the Peloponnese, and it was decided to try to start a pioneer work by sending two preachers with their families to stay for several months, for there was a request from these people for the formation of a church in their area. Thessalonica, though, was to remain the main centre of activity. The work proved hard and sometimes, on a summer's evening, the evangelists would hold meetings out in the courtyards when perhaps thirty to forty Gypsies would attend.

Soon after this, a preacher, Savas, having left the United States, came into contact with some Roms in Greece. He saw their tents by the side of the road and was impressed by their freedom and their life-style. A voice seemed to say to him, 'They also need the gospel but who will go and preach to them?' For quite a while he resisted the appeal, but finally accepted what he believed to be the leading of God. What was he to say to them? What was the gospel he had to proclaim? His first contact with them provided the answer to these questions. His message was simple, pure gospel. 'God loves you,' he told them, 'and sent His Son for you.'

Now Savas too was led towards Thessalonica. A Gypsy woman sought his help and told him that there were several Gypsies at Thessalonica, would he visit them? He did so, visiting, preaching, but apparently failing to make the gospel plain or relevant to them. They just could not understand. Soon after this he heard of the success of some of the French preachers at Alexandria and this gave him courage to continue. But opposition was experienced. The Orthodox priests did their best to discourage Gypsies from listening to the preachers, and the Roms themselves strongly resisted the appeal of the gospel, until at last a miraculous healing changed their minds. So the work went slowly on. Zanellato, working now with a Greek, Stephanos Papadopoulos, worked steadily with small groups of Gypsies, many of whom were living in the direst poverty. The missionaries encountered at first hand the conditions under which many of the Gypsies in Greece lived. There was poverty, idolatry, superstition and instances of violence, drunkenness and drugs, with their attendant horrors. The work was hard and often discouraging but, faithful apostles that they were, they persevered.

In 1975 there was the first real breakthrough. A young Rom was baptised, the first in Greece. The revival had started, they believed, and it would soon become a significant movement. Here we see bold, dedicated, dauntless evangelism over years preceding any marked success. This was often to be the case in the story of the Gypsy Church. 1978 was a decisive year and René could feel the spirit of revival. Even the opposition of the priests had decreased. Perhaps the fact of the charismatic revival around the world had helped the church authorities to see things in a different light, certainly they were showing a more tolerant attitude. Perhaps, too, the evidence of changed lives had its inevitable and telling effect.

Startling too at this time was the conversion of the first Muslim Gypsy, of whom there were thousands in Greece. Who would be able to assess the influence of this man, who was now apparently expressing a desire to serve God in the preaching of the gospel to his fellow Gypsy Muslims, not only in Greece but in Turkey too? For in Turkey there were thousands of Muslim Gypsies; was a new mission field about to open up?

The work took a new dimension in the last months of 1978. The missionaries increased their efforts among the Djambazis and the Roms and actually sited their caravans in the areas in which these people lived, thus identifying themselves closely with them. Soon more than a hundred Gypsies at a time were attending their meetings and listening to the gospel. Again, the Orthodox Church authorities renewed their opposition. They sent special preachers of their own to the Roms to attempt to dissuade them from listening too seriously to these new Gypsy preachers. The Roms, however, would not let themselves be dissuaded and so the police, probably at the instigation of the alarmed ecclesiastical authorities, threatened candidates for baptism with imprisonment and preachers with expulsion.

The advent of a terrifying earthquake which claimed the lives of fifty-four people could have been interpreted as a sign by either side, but the evangelists and their converts did not weaken. Strong in faith and greatly daring, they went ahead with five baptisms and later were to see those people become faithful members of a new church at Seres. In July of that year three Roms from that church attended a convention in Germany. Not only did their presence give great encouragement to those present, it was clearly of tremendous blessing to the Greek Roms themselves and gave them some insight into the character of the movement into which they had entered. To hear them give their testimony in Romany under the great marquee was to believe that the revival was still growing and winning more for Christ.

Certainly this church needed to be guided for there was every sign now that conversions and baptisms were to multiply. René Zanellato settled just outside Thessalonica, teaching the converts while Filia worked among the women and children. Le Cossec himself visited Greece at this critical time, taking Bible study courses, and felt that he was seeing the revival in France all over again when he saw the Holy Spirit fall upon four men in his meeting. It was, he believed, the first Pentecost of the Greek Gypsies. One of these young men was called Lazaros, and was later to become a preacher of the gospel. From this 'mountain-top' experience, he went on to visit Muslim Gypsies in their miserable dwellings, tents constructed by pulling plastic over bent branches, and was to rejoice over the conversion and baptism of one family of this group. Films, especially evangelical films, provided a novel and attractive feature of the work, and the preachers were pleased to see fifty of these Muslim Gypsies watching with keen interest as the gospel was portrayed in this manner. Meanwhile Orthodox opposition was still making itself felt, and the church introduced a system of de-baptising Gypsies who had been influenced by the revival. But the work still continued.

It was felt right at this stage to place the work under the care of a Greek, Stephanos Papadopoulos, who, with Savas and Lazaros, was to take responsibility for evangelism and the care of the churches.

In 1982 they could report that in Thessalonica, a city of 600,000 inhabitants, work was going on successfully in many quarters where Gypsies lived. Meetings were still being held in the homes of Gypsies, but there were hopes of a church being acquired. In fact, Stephanos, with the help of some young Roms, had prepared a centre for worship with financial help from Roms in

Paris. The work was aimed specially at young people from sixteen to twenty-five years of age who, spirit-baptised as they now were, showed keenness in spreading the gospel among their own people. Looking back, René Zanellato would be grateful for the way God had blessed the work of the other preachers and himself. For the work still grew. 1983 would see a church in Thessalonica with Lazaros in charge. It would have forty members, of whom ten had joined in the previous year, it would meet twice weekly and needed the help of two or three Rom preachers.

When someone writes a letter to the Gypsy Church in Thessalonica, there is little doubt that it will remind us startlingly of the one that Paul wrote all those years ago, for the need is the same, the opportunity is the same and the Saviour is the same.

SIX

Fire in the North: Western Europe II

Belgium, the industrialised, densely-populated, bilingual seat of European government, has always presented formidable problems for evangelists outside the Catholic church, for Catholicism is very strong here. It has, though, the distinction of being the first mission field of the Gypsy revival outside France.

A preacher called Roland had made a first contact with Gypsies in the area of Verviers and had seen a real movement among them but, despite gallant though isolated efforts to evangelise other Gypsy families, few results had been achieved. In 1969 the preacher Robert Charpentier undertook the responsibility of co-ordinating all the pioneer work in the country. In Belgium the Gypsies still speak their own language whether they are travelling in the French-speaking Walloon area or in the parts where Flemish is spoken. There are also thousands of Travellers in Belgium who, although they have the same life-style as the real Gypsies, are not in fact Romanies. The isolation in small groups, and the fact that some have abandoned the travelling life-style and have settled, presents the Gypsy evangelist with more than the usual problems. So, up to 1972, the results in Belgium were minimal.

To help to boost the work, a convention was held at Ostend in 1976 and the local workers were thrilled at the number of caravans that gathered from France, Holland and Germany. What was perhaps particularly gratifying to the organisers was the helpfulness of the municipal authorities, who placed at their disposal a site which accommodated 640 caravans. Clearly this convention was a great blessing to all concerned and climaxed with the baptism of twenty-seven people. Onlookers on that day must have wondered what was going on as, the sun sparkling on the sea, a group of Gypsies were immersed in token of their faith, to a chorus of 'Hallelujahs' from their friends. Quite apart from the new baptisms the convention served to bring back several backsliders into the fold. Now though, the work was to sustain a very serious setback. The Gypsy church had been renting a centre in Brussels and that had now been denied them. Undoubtedly this became a great topic of prayer at the convention, but the situation did not alter immediately.

By 1978 the Gypsy mission had made little real progress in Belgium, although Robert Charpentier now had the help of a Rom, Demestre Yojo, who worked largely among the Roms in the country. It could be claimed, however, that some Travellers of non-Gypsy stock had become converted in the course of the years and, to follow this up, a five-day mission was held at Ostend in May 1979. Despite various difficulties in the administration, the organisers experienced the blessing of God and several Gypsies, as well as other Travellers, came to Christ.

In 1981 there was some evidence of activity and perhaps growth, because Roms were now seen to be getting together in lively Christian communities. Hard though this work may have been, slowly as it developed, it is encouraging to discover that a non-Gypsy, converted in Belgium, had married a Gitan Christian woman and had dedicated himself to pioneer work among Manouche Gypsies in Germany. Georges Cruzen spoke German, Manouche, Spanish and French. So, even from this most difficult of areas, the work produced a man who was to be involved in missionary endeavour!

Undoubtedly, as in other lands, the demands of the work in Belgium were very great. Robert Charpentier, soon after his conversion, had asked God to direct him to the country where it was His will he should work, and it was to Belgium that his mind was directed. By 1981 he was still seeing some new baptisms and had established a national committee to organise the work. The work, though, was presenting him with personal problems. His family was becoming an increasing concern and, as his children grew older, it became ever more difficult for him to keep them with him, as his work involved a great deal of travelling. All the family had to accept great sacrifices to enable him to serve the Lord and go to the Gypsy folk of Belgium with the gospel. His work involved not only the spiritual labour of evangelism, but an attempt to help the Gypsies in practical, and often very urgent, matters which were causing them concern. Education, family allowances, sites and similar matters were areas where they needed his help, help he was not slow in giving despite the inroads on his time and the demands of his family.

It was with his usual devotion and care that he organised a convention in May 1982 in the little town of Amay. About 200 caravans grouped around the great marquee and preachers came to help from Belgium itself, France and Holland, all their addresses being translated into the Gypsy tongue. Especially welcome on this occasion were the Roms who, arriving in caravans by the dozen, were grouped under the preacher Demestre Yojo. Clearly he had achieved some real success in his work of evangelism with the Gypsies of this tribe. Work had started among Travellers in 1973 and now they had their own church despite serious opposition from some religious bodies. Some Travellers, several families of them in fact, were present and the workers rejoiced to know that a revival had sprung up among them as the result of the conversion of one of their leaders, a man very well known in Belgium. The baptisms were, as usual, the climax of the convention. What was not so usual though, and all the more welcome for that, was the attendance of the local burgomaster and other leading citizens, who congratulated the Gypsies on their behaviour and invited them to return!

By 1982, the previous setback experienced in Brussels seemed to have been overcome, because the church there now had 150 members, twenty of whom had been baptised in that year, and another church had been established in Brussels. Here, in 1983, there were new conversions among the Travellers and they had their own centre which they attended in increasing numbers. The same year a pastor in Brussels noted how the work among Gypsies was now progressing. He was himself baptising Gypsies and appealed to other pastors to open their churches to this people among whom God was so signally working. So, the work in Belgium not only survives, but grows. But what of its close neighbour, the Netherlands?

The Netherlands must be the only country affected by the Gypsy revival which has had the backing of Royalty!

Once again the impetus has come from France, for the early missionary journeys of the indefatigable French Gypsy preachers included the Netherlands, where there are about 5,000 mainly Manouche Gypsies and non-Gypsy Travellers. Some roots evidently went into the soil for, in 1972, there was a visiting Gypsy in charge of the work aided by Gypsy Christians from the Netherlands itself, and a community had been established near Eindhoven, where about fifty Gypsy or travelling folks had been baptised.

The Netherlands was not without its share of problems as a mission field. The death of a leading preacher was a grievous blow to the whole Gypsy community and the situation was aggravated when a Gypsy boy was killed when a block of concrete fell on him near the site where he was living. Despite this, however, the leaders were determined to plan a new missionary initiative around the country. The Dutch Government provided some well-managed camps for Gypsies who wanted to settle down, and Queen Juliana herself gave regular financial help as well as providing free caravans. In one of these 'Gypsy villages' a church grew up and here it was that Queen Juliana supported the cause by providing a centre for the church. This was at Gerwen, near Eindhoven, where about fifty Manouche Christians would meet every week.

Louis Reinhard, in charge of the work, was able to speak the Manouche language very fluently and with helpers, again from France, had conducted many missions which had resulted in the formation, as at Gerwen, of Christian Gypsy communities. By 1980 the Gerwen community was vibrant and active and owned its own tent for evangelistic purposes, though it was already proving too small to contain the growing numbers who wished to hear the message and take part in the services. Not only this, but it had its own pastor, the Manouche Gypsy Fettela.

Reinhard, known as 'Néné', was converted at the beginning of the Gypsy revival and, by 1962, was one of its leaders. It was as a result of attending a convention in the Netherlands that he felt a call to work there, and by 1981 he was able to see some fruits of the work because there were by then two Manouche churches in the country, more than a hundred had been baptised and elders had been dedicated for the task of preaching the gospel among their own people. Part of Néné's work was to try to teach and prepare these preachers. For this purpose he sought the help of non-Gypsy pastors and was able to give the fledgling preachers a thorough grounding in Biblical knowledge. His fluency in the Manouche language proved invaluable for the church meetings were conducted exclusively in that language, prayers, hymns, sermons and all.

The 1981 convention at Eindhoven was organised by the hardworking Néné. Around the great marquee were grouped caravans of Gypsies who had come from France, Germany and Belgium, as well as from the Netherlands itself. The presence of the President of the Dutch Assemblies of God was very welcome, not merely as it strengthened ties of fellowship, but also for his ability to translate the address of the French-speaking preachers into Dutch. The Sunday saw the usual but wonderful service of baptism.

Looking back, in 1982, on his fourteen years' work in the Netherlands, Néné must have had much for which to thank God. Knowing the superstitious attachment of many Gypsies to religious images he had once told them that their images could neither see, speak nor hear, and he went on to talk of the living Jesus. It was in fact his preaching on that occasion that touched the heart of the Gypsy Fettela, although at that stage he resisted the call of Christ and would not accept the gospel. At a later stage, when the French preachers visited the Netherlands again, Fetella heard the call again and this time he surrendered his life to Christ and started on a life of Christian service as a preacher himself.

By 1983 the membership of the church at Eindhoven had risen to forty, seventeen of whom had joined the church the previous year. The work in the Netherlands had not been easy, but it is now established on a firm basis.

Germany was another problem area for the Gypsy revival. When Clément Le Cossec and his French helpers have to stay in a tramps' shelter for the night because they had no money for anything better, we may be able to understand the way one of the German workers summed it up. It was 'like line fishing', no great catches here, but work demanding patience and a lot of faith.

Lesser Christians, remembering the days of the holocaust and the way in which the Gypsy folk in this land had suffered, might well have hesitated to take the gospel to the country in which those horrific scenes had taken place. Yet this was the land of Luther, the birthplace indeed of the Reformation, and anyway, the Gypsy people had learnt that Christians forgive.

The first real impact was made in 1967 when some Gypsy churches were established, and by 1972 the work was progressing slowly, with about a hundred German Gypsies having been baptised. The work was now under the direction of Gerard Heinzmann who, with the help of some German Gypsies, held tent-missions every year, a work with which, from time to time, the French preachers were also associated. It was on one of these occasions that, lacking money, they had to sleep with tramps. Le Cossec was proud of them, for such was their spirit of dedication that they never grumbled under any conditions. If the work of the French preachers in various countries produced apostolic results it was surely as a direct result of their apostolic dedication! It was a sign of life that a revue in German, *Stimme der Zigeuner* (Voice of the Gypsies) was published, and a sign of health that the 1978 edition contained a great deal of information about the work in India, thus demonstrating a commendable interest in missionary endeavour. As in some other countries, the Gypsy work encountered opposition from local authorities and there was often marked hostility shown to them.

It was when the young German Pentecostalist minister, Gerard Heinzmann, had decided to work full time in this missionary situation that a significant consolidation took place. He it was who saw to the publication of *Stimme der Zigeuner*, which was distributed free to all German-speaking Christians; he saw new converts, the establishment of a lively Gypsy Christian community at Freiburg and, perhaps most significant of all, the raising of some Gypsy preachers.

At a convention of German Roms, held at Mannheim in 1979, the marquee was filled by as many Manouches as Roms, a fact which greatly encouraged all concerned. Among the miraculous cures that were now an accepted, in fact expected, part of such conventions, was that of a Manouche woman who had been paralysed for a year. Overjoyed at her healing, she insisted on dancing, prancing around for the whole of the evening as well as the following day to demonstrate the effectiveness of the cure! An encouraging sign of the times came when the mayor, who had been approached by Heinzmann, authorised them to baptise in the town park. Thousands of Germans viewed this remarkable baptism of sixteen Gypsies on television, whilst hundreds came to watch in person. To seal the happy occasion the mayor himself later visited the convention. An interesting and perhaps significant fact was that, of the sixteen baptised, eight were Roms and eight Manouches. Some considered this a landmark, a sign that the revival in Germany had at last taken off, but there was still a lot to be done in the land that had a Gypsy population of between 30–50,000, many of whom were survivors of the persecution under Hitler. It was always difficult to count the Gypsy population accurately because, although a high proportion had 'settled down', they still tended to be mobile inasmuch as they made seasonal journeys, scattering in small groups throughout the country.

1980 saw the existence of Gypsy churches in seven more towns. Evangelistic missions had been held in various parts of the country and there were now four German Gypsy preachers and six young men preparing for the work, three of whom were Roms who had emigrated from Poland. The revue *Stimme der Zigeuner* was printing 10,000 copies, so the work was getting known and being supported, at least in prayer, by German Christians. In the following year the preachers began adopting the tactic of splitting into two or three groups and evangelising their own people. French preachers, as by now we would expect, came to their aid and they made good use of cassettes, with songs and addresses in both the German and Manouche languages. July 1981 saw a very significant development of the Roms as a race, and not merely of German Roms. This tribe, speaking the Romany language and dispersed throughout Europe into the Americas, Asia, Africa and even Australia and the Pacific areas of the world, would soon be regarded as a high and urgent priority by the Gypsy mission.

A fine site was obtained in Frankfurt by Heinzmann and the Roms arrived, from Germany itself, but also from France, Italy and Sweden. An unusual feature of this convention was that there were not many caravans, for many of the Roms came by cars or on the train! All the hymns and addresses were in the Romany language (its official name is Romanès), but were translated into German for the non-Gypsies present. It proved to be a highly successful convention and was regarded, by the mission, as a pointer to the evangelistic possibilities among the ten million Roms scattered throughout the world.

1982 saw a determined effort in evangelism led by the Gypsy preacher Fardi, who had come from Sweden for this very purpose. In the historic town of Worms, famous for its connection with Luther, a church was to be built for Roms, because so many had settled in that area. So again we see slow but steady progress in a difficult situation. We have dealt, of course, only with Western Germany. Little could be done in an organised way in the Eastern part of this sadly divided land because of the Soviet influence, but despite this it was recorded that in 1982 about a hundred Roms became Christians in the East of Germany. So the Continent of Europe was seeing, in different ways and with varying success, the impact of the Gypsy revival. What of Britain?

Britain presents yet another different situation. The 35,000 or so Gypsies and Travellers in the British Isles do not travel as readily from one country to the other as their Continental cousins, for the Channel has to be contended with. Also the tribal nature of the Continental

Gypsy is not anything like as marked among those of the British Isles. The situation has been complicated, too, in more recent years by the appearance on the English scene of a number of Irish tinkers who do not mix very comfortably with the English Gypsies.

Here again the French Gypsy preachers came to mission but without any really marked success, particularly in the early years, although the situation is changing in a very positive way. In the religious history of Britain there have been determined and often fairly effective attempts to evangelise the Gypsy population. The Salvation Army and the Church Army did a lot in this way and Gypsy converts and evangelists emerged, including the father and the uncles of the famous Gypsy, Rodney Smith, who became a very well-known evangelist on both sides of the Atlantic. An extraordinary man (a friend of his told me that he would stand in her garden with arms outstretched and the birds would settle on his arms), with real preaching ability and a memorable voice, he was used by God to win many people to Christ.

The snag with previous Gypsy work in Britain was that converts were encouraged to leave the Gypsy way of life, which meant that they lost contact with their own folk and were thereby unable to witness effectively to them. Part of the genius of the current Gypsy revival lies in the fact that converts now stay with their people and witness to them as part of the Gypsy scene. In 1972, Jean, the eldest son of Clément Le Cossec, and Loulou Demeter evangelised in England for six months. Going from home to home at first, they stirred interest among the Gypsies and later hired a hall where they saw the conversion of many Gypsies. Le Cossec himself led his team of French preachers and visited many Gypsies and travelling tinkers in London and even in Scotland, but the results had been sparse and he found the work very hard and discouraging.

1978 saw a new initiative in evangelism made by two English Pentecostal pastors and two Gypsy preachers, including Peter Woolford, Chairman of the 'Gypsies for Christ' movement, who was working among Gypsies in South Wales where he lived. No great results seem to have emerged from this brave attempt either, but in 1981 there were signs of hope. Jean Le Cossec (who spoke perfect English, having been trained in America) returned with some French Gypsy preachers and their families. They travelled by caravan to the North of England where they obtained a large tent to use as a church.

One young Gypsy, David Jones, had not spoken to his brother-in-law for many years. Baptised at a previous convention in France, he now had the joy of seeing that brother-in-law accept Christ and there was great joy when, both Christians now, they were reconciled. His wife's conversion and her abandonment of fortune-telling strengthened his faith and he became convinced that God was calling him to serve his own people as an evangelist. To this end both he and his brother-in-law were now hoping to embark on a course of Bible studies to prepare themselves for this work. Later David Jones went to the French Gypsy national convention where he testified that the Lord had helped him surmount every difficulty. Non-Christian Gypsies had assured him that he was heading for distress and poverty (a recurrent theme this) but the Lord had helped him in such a manner as to prove them wrong.

Among the earlier workers for Gypsies one should name Bernard Mends and Fred Farr, secretary and treasurer of 'Gypsies for Christ', and, of course, Mr and Mrs Lamb. Pastor Lamb saw one day a vision in which there was a field of grain ready to be harvested. It meant, he felt sure, that he should volunteer for missionary work overseas, but a pastor friend counselled him against this. The vision came twice more, the third time at the Keswick convention. Then it was that he saw in the vision some Gypsies with caravans in the harvest field. Going to the annual Brough Hill Fair where Gypsies often congregate, he got into conversation with a Gypsy and told him how, as a youth, he had heard Gypsy Smith preach. The Gypsy then told him that he was a descendant of Gypsy Smith. Camping near the Gypsies later, he found they were coming to him with a variety of questions, and so it was he started his work among them. The work was very difficult and, with no visible results forthcoming, he was often discouraged. This was in 1972, but at last he saw a sign of hope with the conversion of young David Jones when the French Gypsies visited England. David had heard the gospel for the first time at the great annual Gypsy fair at Appleby, and it was Pastor Lamb who made the first contact with him, a contact which he kept over a period of six years. Lamb sowed, Jean Le Cossec reaped but God gave the increase.

There is no doubt that, in the last ten years or so, the evangelistic enterprise among Gypsies has proved increasingly successful. This is evidenced, for example, in newspaper articles, quick to notice the unusual phenomenon of religious activity in the Gypsy world. The phenomenon, as one would expect, was noted first in the religious press. In the *Church of England Newspaper* in October 1979 Anne Tyler wrote an article on 'Gypsies for Christ' and described the efforts of the French preachers. She described how the British and Foreign Bible Society was preparing sections of the Bible in the English Romany language and introduced Sid Gray, a Gypsy who had entered the Pentecostal ministry. The *Sunday Times* in 1981 had an article about a Gypsy, Jasper Smith. 'Most of us are Christians,' he is reported as saying, 'I was converted quite recently . . . Jesus was a Gypsy too, you know, He used to beg for food and shelter like we have done.' *The Coventry Evening Telegraph* of March 1982 featured a double church wedding of Gypsies conducted by a Pentecostal pastor who had recently been consulted by some fifty Gypsies about the Christian faith. Cliff, one of the bridegrooms, was reported as saying, 'We have a new way of life now and it's wonderful. I used to drink fourteen pints of beer a night and smoke constantly, but I can honestly say that is all in the past now . . . all we want now is to help others in our community join the Christian faith'. An Epsom paper, the *Advertiser*, with the headline 'Church comes to the Gypsies', described hopes to set up a permanent church base at the Cox Lane Gypsy site, whilst the *Guardian* of July 1983 tells of some apprehension in Derbyshire at the prospect of an 'invasion' of Christian Gypsies for a convention. This is probably the convention reported by *The Times* the following month. It had been held on a Derbyshire farm and the Gypsies had provided their own accommodation, church (a 200 person tent) and baptismal font (a plastic inflatable pool). 'The last was much used on Sunday,' they report, 'when twenty of the Gypsies, aged seventeen to forty, were "born again" by being immersed in it.' This is the evidence of the press, but I have further personal evidence.

In the summer of 1982 I attended a Department of Education and Science course on Gypsy education, where I was introduced to a young teacher from Lincolnshire. Unaware of the Gypsy revival movement, she had noticed, with some astonishment, the difference in the lives of the Gypsy families she knew and whose children she had taught. The husbands had stopped getting drunk and were treating their families much better. Some Gypsy children were even asking to be taught to read, so that they could read the Bible! Another teacher from Yorkshire had noticed the same sort of thing, testimony this to the work of the gospel among the Gypsies.

When I attended a similar course two years later, what had been known to only a few was now fairly generally known. Some teachers of Gypsies were deploring the fact that, at the same time as the course, a convention was being held for Gypsies in the Wolverhampton area. I heard news of the revival amongst Gypsies in the South-East and in East Anglia, and the revival was mentioned as a factor to be taken into consideration by a visiting speaker. On my return home I heard, in conversation with Jimmy and Doris, of someone looking for premises for a Gypsy church in Bristol, whilst they themselves had been approached to mission among Gypsies in Yorkshire.

Another significant advance in 1984, in line with a move to link up with the Assemblies of God that has characterised recent years, was a meeting between leaders of the Gypsy movement in England and the French, as a result of which a national council was set up to further the work.

'They have an easy life, all, in fact that they could desire, so why accept Jesus into their life?' 'Swiss Gypsies are rejected by society but, Glory to God, are accepted by Him.' Those two quotations about the Gypsies in Switzerland just about sum up the two major facts concerning them. They share in the general affluence of the country, but, perhaps because of the standards of that favoured land, are indeed often rejected. It is difficult to say for sure how many Gypsies there are in Switzerland, at least as far as real Romanies are concerned, for, as in Belgium, there are also non-Gypsy travelling folk who are regarded by the evangelical Gypsy movement as being part of their responsibility. In total the whole travelling population could number thousands.

The origins of the revival in Switzerland are not clear but it could be claimed, in 1972, that many had accepted Jesus as their Saviour and certain Christian communities had been established in a few cities. Once again the evangelistic drive and groundwork had come from the French preachers, one of the results of whose work was the emergence of a few native Swiss preachers.

Contacts had been made in Switzerland as early as 1958 and some families were reached, but it was not until the preacher Debarre Madou committed himself to remain in the country for three years to do missionary work that things really happened. During those three years seventy Gypsies were baptised and some of the communities were established. Here again we see outreach from the Gypsy church to others. Frequently the Gypsy preachers were invited to conduct missions in the Protestant churches of the country and they were always warmly welcomed and appreciated.

It was some measure of the frailty and difficulty of the work in this country that the work was placed under the responsibility of the French movement as part of planning for further, country-wide efforts of evangelisation. The Gypsy preacher Maille Bittel reported, in 1981, a very fruitful evangelistic campaign. He concentrated mainly on German-speaking Switzerland where the local ministers welcomed and indeed helped him. Acknowledging with gratitude the commitment to the Swiss work of two French Gypsy preachers, he comments on the difficulty of tracing the 'Travellers', most of whom had now ceased to travel! A new large marquee had been acquired though, the work of the mission was growing and, especially among the non-Gypsy Travellers, doors were opening. Gratifying too was the fact that some 'backsliders' were returning to Christ and a few seemed likely to become preachers. To gather twenty to twenty-seven caravans together for a convention in this very difficult area was, he felt, something of an achievement and he was grateful to the Lord for enabling him to do it.

A résumé of the work in 1982 deplored the spiritual hardness of the Travellers and the Gypsies. Their apathy, it was felt, was in no small measure due to the affluence of their lives, and this fact, it was believed, could well account for the slow growth of the revival. Nevertheless about a thousand had been reached with the gospel and about a hundred had given their lives to Christ. From 1979 to 1982, in fact, the work of evangelism among Swiss Gypsies had indeed grown. A fairly new technique of evangelism had developed in this country. Large conventions had not proved appropriate and a sort of 'rolling' convention had emerged. The evangelist would go out and, *en route*, gather caravans and people. For example, a recent evangelistic tour had started with seven caravans. After two weeks of mission with the marquee the number grew to fifteen. Every day new Travellers joined with their caravans so that when they reached the end of this tour they numbered thirty-seven caravans. Many new young people were among the converts and it was especially among them that the Holy Spirit worked to such great effect. People were baptised and people were healed. So, in this difficult terrain for evangelism, the work was growing.

1984 saw a reorganisation of the work to try to extend and improve the work of evangelism. Maille Bittel assumed the presidency in co-operation with two French preachers, Antoine Reinhardt and Djimey Meyer. Circumstances in the country affecting the life of the Gypsies and the Travellers seemed, to the mission, to be making the work of evangelism even more urgent, and so they called on the churches of Switzerland to make a determined effort to take up the challenge of the Gypsies as yet unevangelised. The steady growth of the work and the increasing support of the Swiss churches bodes well for the future of the mission.

When we think of Gypsies we usually associate them with Western Europe: the spectacular flamenco dancers of Spain, or with Eastern Europe: the swarthy violinists of the Balkan States. Certainly we rarely imagine them in Scandinavia but, of course, there are Gypsies in those northern lands, though not on the same scale as in other countries. You would perhaps find 5,000 in Finland, as in Sweden, though they are fewer in number in Norway and Denmark. The greatest contrast one would note with regard to the Gypsy population in those countries is the treatment they tend to receive there, compared with their lot in many other areas. The Scandinavian countries certainly seem more enlightened in their treatment of minorities, and certainly in Sweden great trouble is taken to care for the Gypsy population and to educate them (superbly produced books are published with this in mind), although gentle pressure is exerted to persuade them to settle down.

Finland, hauntingly beautiful land of lakes and forests, and near neighbour of the great Soviet Union, contains Gypsies who still observe the basic rules and customs of their tribes. Blood-feuds are not unknown among this people, to whom the revival came as early as 1954. By 1972 about 300 Gypsies were converted and baptised and they would be proud of the fact that a young Finnish Gypsy, Hermann, was sent to England to learn the language with a view to missionary service. At this stage a couple by the name of Virjo were carrying out a dedicated ministry among the Gypsy population, a ministry which they, though not themselves Gypsies, were to continue with great fidelity.

By 1978 another Finnish non-Gypsy Christian, by the name of Mattaison, was able to attend a convention in France, thus himself receiving encouragement and publicising the work in Finland. New offers of Christian service were being made by converted Gypsies, he was to report, and that year too saw the arrival of the indomitable team of French Gypsy preachers whose mission in this land was to prove a great success. Other churches in Finland were now showing practical interest in Gypsies, who were grateful for the Lutheran church's provision of a residential home for Gypsy children. The Assemblies of God invited six Gypsy preachers to their convention and were thrilled and impressed by the witness they gave.

One preacher from the Gypsy community in Finland was, in 1980, studying at a Bible College in Dallas in America. Speaking the Romany language himself, he was able also to teach it to others and felt a call to work on the immense mission field which was now increasingly exercising the mind of the movement: the ten million Roms as yet unevangelised. Two of his colleagues were preparing for missionary work in Spain and India, so now the Gypsy people of Finland were themselves producing missionaries, always a healthy sign!

The high respect with which the Gypsy preachers were regarded by the other churches of the country is evidenced by the fact that their services were keenly sought as missioners for special evangelistic campaigns. Gypsies are often very musical and frequently possessed of magnificent voices (like the great Gypsy Smith in former days), and their singing brought a great deal of blessing to the local churches, so much so that they made many cassettes of evangelical songs which became very popular.

Little is known of the work in Denmark where, compared with other countries like Sweden or Finland, there are few Gypsies. This of course did not daunt the French preachers, who made evangelistic visits to the country as did preachers from Sweden and Norway. It is also known that a very worthwhile work was done among the Gypsies by a Christian woman, one of the glorious band of often unnamed, sometimes unknown, workers who persevere with a fidelity that honours their Lord.

The work among the comparatively few Gypsy folk of Norway proved difficult and there were few conversions, although hopes were high that some of the younger converts might offer themselves for the work of the ministry. A curious thing happened in this country, which was reported in The Press at the beginning of 1981. Someone gave a lift to a hitch-hiker who sat in the back of the car and proceeded to tell the driver that the Lord was coming soon! The driver, not surprisingly, was puzzled by what had been said and turned to question the hitch-hiker, only to discover there was no one behind him! This apparently was not an isolated incident and happened to a number of drivers, not only in Norway but also apparently in the United States. Whatever its explanation, it reinforced, among the Gypsies, their firmly held view that the return of the Lord was imminent, and it certainly served to strengthen the dedication of Norwegian Gypsy Christians. At about this time also, several Manouche families were converted as a result of a miraculous healing. Perhaps it was this growth that made the Norwegian Gypsies express a wish, in 1983, for a church of their own. With this they coupled a plea for a Rom preacher to minister to them.

Of the Scandinavian countries, it is perhaps Sweden that has seen the greatest activity by revivalists working with the Gypsy community. This country of eight million inhabitants had always shown a comparatively sympathetic attitude to Gypsies, and had welcomed in recent years some 5,000 Gypsies of the Rom tribe. Like most Roms, they had previously lived in Eastern Europe and had come to hospitable Sweden from Poland, Russia, Czechoslovakia, Hungary or Yugoslavia, although a few had emigrated from Spain and France. This influx of Gypsies then was comparatively modern, and only about 800 had lived in Sweden for a matter of generations. It was to this Rom community that another Rom came to minister and evangelise.

Atanasio Fardi was a Rom of the Kalderash tribe (a numerous tribe speaking Romany and given the name *Kalderash*, meaning 'coppersmith', to show their well-known proficiency in working in metal). He was converted in 1961 and had been a mission evangelist for five years when, in 1974, he moved to Sweden with his wife and children. It took him six months before he could obtain a visa and he spent this period in the special 'welcome' camps that Sweden had set up for immigrants, where he learned the Swedish language. This could not have been easy for a man of his background but he persevered in his study of the language and then went on to a course of biblical studies.

Fardi preached and witnessed to the Gypsy folk of Sweden wherever in the country he could find them, a mission which involved him in a weekly round trip of some 2,000 kilometres or more. Soon some 200 Gypsies were attending his meetings, people were being converted and miraculous cures were reported. One of the new immigrant groups of Roms who had been in the country for only eight years responded warmly to his ministry and received the word of God with joy. One formerly Czech Gypsy, now living in Sweden, requested Fardi to pray for her son still in Czechoslovakia, who had gone blind. Fardi prayed as requested, and to such effect that when the son was miraculously cured the baffled Czech authorities accused him of having falsely claimed to have gone blind simply to claim a pension! Little wonder then that the fervour of some of the converts was such that they were happy to worship at meetings which lasted from six in the evening to eleven thirty at night, and also that some young men were coming forward and offering themselves for the service of the ministry.

Here, as in Finland, the Lutheran Church proved friendly to the new movement and its new converts, to the extent of lending them one of their churches in which to worship. Now the number of converts was mounting, as were the vocations to the ministry of young men who responded with enthusiasm and gratitude to the Bible studies which Clément Le Cossec conducted for them in 1980. The few days he spent with them clearly encouraged them to pursue further studies along these lines at the Pentecostal church 'Filadelfia'. The Gypsies also used their musical talents to the full and formed a very fine choir which was in great demand. The Pentecostalists also helped with the publication, in Swedish, of the international news magazine of the movement *Life and Light*.

As the movement took shape, Le Cossec, always clearly and sensitively aware of the importance of training young men for the ministry, undertook further work among them. Over a period of a month, they met several times a week to study the word of God. Le Cossec taught them about the church, the ministries, spiritual gifts, preaching, the future life, the return of Christ and other Christian doctrines. There were now eight budding Rom preachers, all of whom had attended school in Sweden and some of whom had studied English over a period of years. The work, though, was not entirely without its problems even at this stage, and there was a temporary difficulty when, as a result of the misleading teaching of a Rumanian Gypsy preacher, the church had to be shut. This man had based his erroneous teaching on visions and not on the word of God. For a people prone to visions this must have presented a perplexing problem, but the lesson was learnt, the errors corrected and the church eventually reopened.

The public of Sweden was now becoming aware of what was happening, as a result of a great service televised from the Filadelfia church and showing the baptism of several Gypsies. Not similarly publicised, but of great importance, was the task of dealing with some 3,000 Gypsies from Finland who were now immigrating into Sweden. Here the Swedish and Finnish preachers could usefully combine their efforts in what could prove to be a significant and productive cross-fertilisation of the two.

June 1982 saw the first European convention of Roms at Lille in France. Among those attending this convention, at which all the proceedings were in Romany, was a group from Sweden who felt greatly encouraged by the fellowship they experienced. The strength and growth of the movement in Sweden was seen the following year, because Fardi could report a Gypsy church in Stockholm, led by himself and attended by eighty Roms, ten of whom had been recently converted.

By 1984 it could be confidently claimed that the Gypsy church in Sweden was growing and it was especially pleasing to report that several young men, including a former drug addict, had recently been converted. Young preachers were still firm in their vocation and evangelistic campaigns were being planned, not only for various parts of Sweden itself, but also for Copenhagen. There are now two Gypsy churches in Stockholm. One is for Roms from France, Spain, Belgium or Italy who have emigrated to Sweden, and the other for Gypsies born in the country, this attached to the Filadelfia Pentecostal church.

A new and important development had taken place at this time. A gathering of Christian leaders including Atanasio Fardi, now President of the Gypsy mission in Sweden, and Clément Le Cossec had agreed to set up, with the help of Swedish Christians, a European Gypsy Centre in Paris. The object would be to facilitate contact with the ten million Roms in Europe as yet unevangelised. It would be a centre of Bible training, a Gypsy church and the hub of a variety of evangelistic activities, all in the Romany language.

So, here in Sweden the revival was outward-looking, with an eye to the 'lands of the East', as the Gypsies called Eastern Europe, home of the Roms.

SEVEN

Behind the Iron Curtain

Turning to Eastern Europe from the open society of the West, we are in another world. Here there is suspicion, state persecution, secrecy and the deadening hand of atheistic Communism. Reports of the work from this part of Europe have necessarily to be cautiously phrased, names must sometimes be suppressed, photos not shown for fear of reprisals upon those who feature in them. The background then seems grey, but behind the grey there is an extraordinary light, for this part of Europe has, in recent years, been the scene of a great religious revival among the general population. Largely unpublicised but powerful and active, the work of the Spirit has influenced a great number of people, not least the six million Gypsies who live in Eastern Europe. Because of the conditions in which the work among Gypsies has had to be conducted and the cautious manner in which it has had to be reported, the progress of the Gypsy revival here has been told usually in short, guarded and staccato reports, almost like bulletins coming in from the battle front. This is how the story will be told in this chapter.

In 1972 the Gypsy movement made its battle plans for a worldwide offensive of evangelistic enterprise. Among the projects envisaged was the sending of workers to Yugoslavia. They had already had contact with several Gypsies in this land where some two million Gypsies lived, some Orthodox by religion, some Muslim, although this religious colouring was more often than not a matter of form. The hope was to try to establish some evangelical Christian communities among these people, some of whom were well educated, technicians, engineers and the like. Poland, too, had seen missionary efforts by the Gypsy movement and some Gypsies in this land had in fact been won for Christ. An encouraging fact had been the help offered to these new converts by Polish non-Gypsy Christians and their pastors, but the real need was for one or two Gypsy preachers from France, though this seemed a forlorn hope at that time. Czechoslovakia, Hungary and Bulgaria had also been reached with the witness of the gospel and Gypsies there had heard the good news.

Rumania, which had seen perhaps the greatest effect of the religious revival that had spread throughout Eastern Europe, had been the scene of the conversion of some Gypsies, and when Gypsy missionaries arrived they learnt to their astonishment and delight that some 2,000, perhaps even more, were converted and were now members of Christian communities. In this land there are whole villages peopled solely by Gypsies with, in some cases, a population of as many as 10,000. What proved so sad in the eyes of the missionaries was that, quite untypically, the President of the Assemblies of God gave little support to their team in their attempt to witness to the Gypsies. Two preachers who had taken it upon themselves as a vocation to concentrate upon the Gypsy folk had been imprisoned and had only been released on condition that they no longer concerned themselves with Gypsies. One of these preachers, Rascol, was permitted to leave Rumania and he and his family were granted political asylum in Austria. Other preachers, however, remained and one of them could declare that he was prepared for arrest, torture or death in Christ's cause. Certainly God had blessed this man's faith and work for, in collaboration with the official churches he was attracting some 600 Gypsies to worship.

In 1977 there was news of a revival in Hungary among

Gypsies on the Russian border, as a result of the witness of Hungarian Christians. No place-names could be given for fear of creating difficulties for the Christians in these areas, but the work would certainly continue. At the same time Yugoslavia now had three lively Christian Gypsy communities and the local, anonymous Gypsy preacher was understandably encouraged as he had also obtained permission to open places of worship.

Poland was in the news again the following year as Loulou had carried out missions there and several Gypsies had been baptised. Non-Gypsy ministers seemed to show little interest in the work among the Gypsies and there was clearly need for more missionary work. In Czechoslovakia, Hungary, Bulgaria and Rumania missionary journeys had been made, some meetings being held clandestinely, and there were ten preachers in those countries. Rumania now had some 5,000 converted Gypsies, most of whom were attached to the Assemblies of God. A new revival was taking place in Hungary, and the witness of the gospel had been taken, by Gypsy preachers, to the South and North of Russia itself.

In Yugoslavia there was more liberty and the Gypsy preacher Millo, himself a Rom, now had responsibility for five Gypsy communities which he had founded. This young man had been converted in Vienna, when French Roms were missioning there. Baptised at the Strasbourg convention, he was now working among his own people. That same year a brother from Eastern Europe wrote of the joy of seeing a revival among a tribe of Roms somewhere on the Russian frontier and photos taken in Eastern Europe among Christian Gypsies added further evidence to the growth of the movement.

Still in Yugoslavia, discussion with the Gypsy pastor, Mio, led to the acquisition of a city centre for Gypsy meetings. This was necessary because in this country meetings were forbidden without the existence of such a centre. The new centre was capable of accommodating a hundred Gypsies and would prove of great value, especially in view of the fact that several baptisms were envisaged. Mio, with a minister of the Reformed Church of Hungary, had been able to attend the 1979 convention at Ennordres and gave first hand accounts of the work in the lands of Eastern Europe.

First hand, too, was the report given by Clément Le Cossec the same year. In Bucharest, capital of Rumania, the Rumanian Christian who was guiding the missionary party happened to mention that a family of Christian Gypsies lived nearby, and suggested a visit. The family did not know of this intended visit that was so dramatically to change their lives. The father of the family had now suffered for a long time from a dreadfully painful heart condition. It seemed to get worse, the pain more intense and his chances of recovery, or even survival, seemed minimal. He had decided to wait two more days and then end it all. The mother was delighted to see the missionaries, excited in fact, for only that morning she had asked the Lord to send some servants of God to pray for her husband's healing. They went in to see the sick man and it was clear that he was suffering dreadfully, although neither the missionaries nor his wife and family knew of his pact with death. After talking to him about the promises of the Scriptures, they anointed him with oil in the name of the Lord and prayed for his healing. Returning from their mission two days later, they went back to find out how he was. He was up and about, totally cured and joyfully witnessing to the power of the living Lord. Later he told them of what he had intended. His suicide had been planned for Thursday, the following day. Now he was well and rejoicing!

By now many of the 500,000 Gypsies in Rumania were converted and several had become preachers. Some were members of the official churches but many had to meet in secret. One of the 'underground' preachers was summoned to the police station where he was reminded that he had no right to bring people together to speak of God and the Bible. The Gypsy, knowing the official's interest in soccer, pointed out that he obviously invited his friends to his home and, equally obviously, the conversation was about football. As for him, he got his friends together and they talked about the word of God. Everybody, he solemnly assured the official, talks about what interests them. He was allowed to carry on!

Shamu was one of the best Rumanian evangelists. He started by gathering a few friends around him for prayer, although he had already been committed to prison for this faith. Then it was that the Spirit of God really started to work among this growing group of Gypsies, so he bought a larger house to make into a church. Miraculous cures took place and the congregation grew to 1,000! The Communist Party demanded that it be closed, but Shamu refused. He was arrested and sentenced to six months in prison, where they put him in the psychiatric ward. Here he would really have gone mad had he swallowed the pills they tried to make him take. When his wife protested she was badly beaten, but still their faith held firm. Eventually Shamu was released but had to leave the country for America, and his church was closed.

Missionaries were later to be held up at the frontier of Rumania for two hours as their vehicles were examined meticulously for hidden Bibles, but they were able to enjoy, late as they were, taking part in a service which, starting at nine in the morning, was to go on to four in the afternoon! This in a place full to overflowing, where only sixteen years before a mere twenty Gypsies met in a house. This was now a lively church, very charismatic, and the worship included the washing of feet, while the taking of the bread and the wine were both followed by songs and sermons. Men and women were separated during the service. The spiritual life was intense, if somewhat mystical and, probably as a result of the lack of Bibles and scriptural teaching, great emphasis was placed upon the gifts of the Spirit. The growth of the work, though, was greater even than it had been in France because, for 50,000 Pentecostal Christians in France there are three times that number in Rumania, a country with half the population.

Hungary offers more liberty and a Reformed pastor had a congregation of 500, of whom 80 per cent were Gypsies.

This country has 500,000 Gypsies, who appear to be related to the French Manouche. In 1981 the National Radio broadcast the testimonies of Manouche Christians in their church situated just on the Russian border. This lively programme was beamed out at a peak period. The same year saw Gypsies from other lands helping the Rumanian preacher Radulesko. Turned out of his own country, the Rumanian authorities had said he could return if he appeared on television and said that God did not exist, which he refused to do.

Persecution was reported in Yugoslavia as two preachers on a mission, where they saw the outbreak of revival, were arrested. They were put in prison as was the Rom, Mio, and one preacher, Antoine, and his young son were badly beaten.

Heinzmann, co-ordinator of the work among the Gypsies of the Eastern European countries, visited Rumania. Refused permission to take food and clothes to Rumanian Gypsies, he had to leave them in Hungary. Finally able to visit Rumania he reported, in 1982, that there was a new breath of revival among Gypsies in the area of Bucharest, a revival bringing spiritual freedom to a people who, a hundred years before, had been slaves and who had been forbidden to speak the Gypsy language.

So, despite persecution and the need for secrecy, the revival in Eastern Europe has progressed at an astonishing rate.

EIGHT

Into the New World

The Gypsies and the Jews have often been compared. Indeed it has sometimes been suggested that the Gypsies were the lost tribes of Israel. Apart from their dispersion and the persecution common to both, however, there is little resemblance. The great difference is that the Jews have a well-documented history and an authoritative Holy Book, whereas the Gypsies' past is little known and, although they have their customs and taboos dating back from their Indian animistic religion, they have frequently taken on the religious hue of whatever countries they have found themselves in. But both groups have travelled and perhaps we should not be surprised to find Gypsies in the New World.

Centuries ago Gypsies were sent from France to Louisiana and from Spain to South America and they have lived in those lands ever since. It was a Gypsy Christian woman, one of the million Gypsies living in the United States of America, who had the vision of the European revival. She saw a great number of her fellow-Gypsies being brought to Christ but could not reach them because of a great stretch of water between them and her. We can imagine her joy when she finally learnt exactly what her vision had meant, and that thousands of Gypsies on the Continent of Europe were, in fact, crowding into the Kingdom of God.

1954 saw the 'little cloud . . . like a man's hand', a minor revival among a family of Manouche Gypsies in

Nebraska which did not, however, develop greatly or make any marked impression outside of that area. In 1963 Clément Le Cossec with his son Jean (who was to study for the Pentecostal ministry in the States), visited the country and toured as many Gypsy centres as he could, sometimes with Loulou Demeter, an experienced veteran of evangelistic enterprise.

Loulou Demeter returned to the States in 1972 and was based in Newark, New Jersey, a location that was to prove an important centre for the spread of the gospel among Gypsies in the States. Part of the challenge that confronted him was the problem of adjusting himself to living in an apartment building, especially on the third floor! This, however, he faced and, strange to him as it was, managed to cope with it. A real work had started at Los Angeles with the conversion and baptism of twenty-one Gypsies, and now God was to work in Newark. The problem of accommodation was a serious one, for at first they had no place to meet for worship, no centre of evangelism, but later they were able to secure premises and, greatly daring in faith, obtained sixty-five chairs to use in it!

1972 was an eventful year in the story of the work of revival and evangelism among Gypsies in the United States, for it also saw the addition to the team of Derek Tipler, an English Gypsy, University educated, who assumed considerable responsibility for the work, especially in the field of Bible translation. The Wycliffe Society charged him with the translation of the New Testament into the Romany language, an important step indeed, and at a strategic moment for the work among Gypsies in America. For Gypsies were now pouring into the country, and the need for this kind of translation was paramount. Prominent too in the translation work, and great supporters of Christian work among American Gypsies, were Ruth Morrow and her husband, who had worked among Gypsies in Portland.

The attempt to read the New Testament in the

Romany language, with the aid of cassettes from the Bible Society, has been, for me, a most interesting and fruitful experience. Full of insights into the language and the attitudes of the Gypsies. The Gypsies who read the extracts from the Gospels are careful to say, as they read the introduction to the actual text, '*Me penav* – this is me speaking' and then, before they actually start on the text, '*E Bibla penel* – the Bible says'.

When reading the parable of the Good Samaritan, I realised that the Gypsy language has no word meaning 'neighbour'. How can nomads have neighbours? So they use words meaning 'friend' or 'the next' to try to express the meaning. For 'repent' they use the word *ambol* which means 'turn', surely an accurate rendering of the basic New Testament meaning of the word! The word they use for 'pray', from the root word *drab*, is also used, in the Romany tongue, for 'poison'. Here we see the common idea of the supernatural expressed in different ways in the same word, for the widespread belief that Gypsies would poison folk is clearly linked with the popular view of their occult powers.

In the States the Gypsies have their 'kings', and it was one such 'king' who gave the Morrows permission to learn the Gypsy language. They knew this would be useful for their work among the Gypsies when they saw their joyous reaction to tapes and records made by a Gypsy preacher in Europe. So their work went on alongside that of Derek Tipler although they realised that there was one great drawback, for about 90 per cent of the Gypsies in America were illiterate, and literacy teaching was an urgent priority.

Just about the time that all this was happening, the gospel was being spread in a manner perhaps unusual in this country, but in the classic way, if we remember the early days of the revival in France. The Gypsies who had been converted and baptised in Los Angeles had gone on the move and were testifying to their new-found faith in Sacramento, New York or wherever their wanderings took them. So the work grew in a natural, spontaneous New Testament way. Certainly five years later Stevo Demeter (a preacher who had been instrumental in the work in Mexico) was holding meetings twice weekly in two townships on the outskirts of New York with increasing numbers attending. Roms were now moving into the area from Los Angeles and Houston and (again like the early converts in France) were using the telephone, this time to express their keen desire for evangelistic cassettes. Clearly too they were learning to read the Bible more and more, and told Stevo that they would pay his fare to go and teach them about the Lord.

In 1978 Le Cossec could feel that the revival was now really under way. The first convention had already taken place in 1977 and a second one would take place at the end of May 1978 at Carlinville, in Ohio. Encouraging as things were seeming, it is surprising that, at this stage, after all this work, there were still only about 100 converts. Hopes were high, though, that the Spirit would bless and increase the work. Traditionally and according to New Testament practice, women 'kept silence' in the churches. They were allowed, indeed encouraged, to testify but not to preach. But they could have sons who preached and maybe their testifying bordered very closely on preaching as, I suspect, was the case with Sister Camelia, proud mother of two preacher sons, who was typical of many women in this male-orientated church. The visit of this remarkable European Gypsy woman made a great impression upon the American Gypsies.

1980 saw evangelistic campaigns at Lafayette and other cities, and in 1983 the first efforts were made to create a church for the Roms of America and a year-long campaign was launched in Los Angeles. This seems to have been a success for, under the leadership of Sam Mitchell (Savka), a fairly recent convert, the church grew there to 700 members. Things were moving, and sizeable communities of evangelical Gypsies were springing up in

Chicago, Houston and Boston among other places. So great was the progress at this time that, whereas in 1978 there were only 100 converts, now about 3,000 were converted and baptised and there were forty Gypsy preachers!

1983, preceded as it had been by about five years of revival, had also seen the Travellers (non-Gypsy nomads) touched by the gospel, a fact which Le Cossec noted with pleasure on a visit to the States that year. Always ready to venture into something new to further the work among his beloved Gypsies, Le Cossec and his wife had taken a course in Romany at a Paris University and he delighted to speak to the American Gypsies in their own language!

Typical of the health of the movement in the States now was the church at Los Angeles where Savka was pastor. This was the biggest of the Rom churches, where sometimes 700 Roms would attend. At Houston the pastor, Miller Mitchell (Milano) was in charge of a church at the crossroads. Many Roms passed through as they crossed the country on their travels, but it was, of course, difficult to sustain a settled work among the Gypsies or the Travellers who also attended. At Miami there was Pastor Brown, who had left his own church five years previously to work among Gypsies, and was now linked with the Assemblies of God who, he claimed, were a sort of 'umbrella' protecting the Gypsies. They would still retain their own identity, but the Assemblies could help in preparing and training preachers. New York had seen the baptism of some 500 Roms and desperately needed a Rom pastor.

The Los Angeles church of which Savka was the pastor was a real missionary church for it had sent 1,200 cassettes in Romany to Roms throughout the United States, Mexico, Peru and Venezuela. This help was very much to the point for now South America was seeing a Gypsy revival of its own!

Mention has briefly been made of Mexico and the work there of Stevo Demeter, for the work of God amongst Gypsies was going on in Central and South America as well as in the North.

In 1981 the pastor Lauriol was given the job of co-ordinating the work in South American countries including Brazil and Venezuela as well as Argentina, which was to be the scene of the greatest activity and success. In 1983 the preacher Diego Jimenes, charged with the task of co-ordinating the evangelisation of his own Gitan people, went to South America where, of course, many Gitan Gypsies were living. He reported that in Brazil he held daily meetings and about 100 Gitans came to hear the word of God. Almost all of these were converted and several of them experienced miraculous healings. Among this group were a family of Portuguese Gypsies, the mother of whom was delivered from her bondage to spiritualism. The Gypsies of Brazil were requesting a pastor from Spain to instruct them in Christian matters, so it was decided, at the convention in Madrid, to send the Gitan pastor Alfredo to mission there.

1984 could report a revival in Peru. This arose because a young Rom Gypsy, Miguel Valodia, formerly an atheist, had attended, almost by chance, an evangelistic meeting addressed by Stevo Demeter in Mexico. Touched by the gospel, he fell to his knees and yielded his life to Christ. Stevo, perhaps sensing the potential in this man, gave him regular Bible teaching over the space of two months, after which Valodia left for Peru. There he continued his studies with the help of pastors of the Assemblies of God. For a year he studied and prayed, fasting twice a week. Then he started to evangelise his own Rom people in Peru. He founded the Gypsy church in Lima, baptised 180 Gypsies of the Rom tribe and could report a 'waiting-list' of 120 candidates for baptism! Of these converts eighteen were already feeling a sense of vocation for the ministry, and there were some who decided to go to Argentina to evangelise their people there.

With the growing work in Argentina and converstions among the Gypsies in Colombia, Venezuela and Brazil, the South American continent was being blessed indeed. The indefatigable Stevo, accompanied by the preacher Kolia, was due to visit Peru the following March, so the work there promised to grow. Indeed it did, for in 1984 300 baptisms were reported, twelve men had dedicated themselves to the work of preaching and Christian communities had been created in Venezuela and Chile, whilst in Colombia many Roms had been converted. Mexico, Stevo's first mission field, had now seen 100 Roms baptised and what was to become the start of a real revival.

There are tens of thousands of Gypsies in South America, and of these some 35,000 are in Argentina, a country seven times the size of France. Here the Gypsy work has really swung into action. It was in 1969 that Lauriol started work among the Gypsies, particularly among their children. By 1972 though, he had his fair share of difficulty and discouragement because, after two years hard work, he could only claim that one family of Gypsies had been won for Christ. Sometimes he could get about thirty Gypsies to his meetings, but he felt the need of the help of a Gypsy preacher who could communicate more readily with his fellow-Gypsies.

In 1973 Clément Le Cossec visited Lauriol in Buenos Aires and put him in contact with Spanish Gitans called '*Calos*' ('the blacks'). Le Cossec told him, 'In a little while, with the Calos you will have a church of more than 200 Gitans.' This proved to be prophetic indeed because afterwards, starting a work of evangelism at Rosario, he felt revival was really starting. From the very beginning the Holy Spirit made Himself known, and drug addicts and alcoholics were freed from their bondage, a young girl was healed and there were real signs of repentance. With Christians at Rosario wanting his help, he felt torn between that place and the opportunities of Buenos Aires where the number of converts continued to grow and where he had the immense joy of baptising his first Gitan.

In 1977 a Gypsy preacher was sent to Argentina. He was Pako, whose mission was primarily to train Gitan preachers in Argentina. Better educated academically than most of his folk, his simple style seemed suited to the need as he sought to teach at a deep, spiritual level.

Lauriol, having spent some time in Algeria, was in 1978 once again in Argentina. Previously his contact had mainly been with Roms, but now he had been in touch with Gitans and had seen conversions from both tribes, aided no doubt by the French preachers. At the European convention in 1979 he was able to report on the progress of the work, especially among the Roms resident in Buenos Aires where a Christian community was taking shape. Hopes were high of sending two Rom preachers from France to assist in the work.

Welcome fruit came, after so many years of apparent barrenness, as 150 Roms from Buenos Aires and other cities took part in a mission which culminated in a service of baptism in the river. More and more Roms were being converted now and other baptisms were taking place, including baptisms in the Holy Spirit.

The advantage of a common tribal language is seen in the way preachers were virtually interchangeable across national boundaries. This showed clearly, too, the wisdom of the important decision to work tribally, taken at the 1979 convention. Loulou and Fardi (both veterans of other countries but speaking the tribal language) visited Argentina and went to the frontier of Uruguay where some Gypsy families were baptised. This group was surprised by the visit as they were only then listening to Bible studies which Lauriol had made, as well as a cassette by Loulou himself, which had been sent from France!

In 1982 some Roms who had gone from Buenos Aires

to Barcelona sought help from Kolia in their preparation and then returned to Argentina to witness and evangelise. Lauriol, in the meantime, had obtained permission to appear on television for an hour with the message of the gospel and the witness of Gypsy preachers. 1983 could show fifty members in the church in Argentina who badly needed a Rom preacher, whilst in 1984 there now existed at Rosario an evangelical community of forty Spanish-speaking Gitans. So the work progresses in the New World.

NINE

Back to the roots

An invitation to a wedding, from India! I received it on a Tuesday and the wedding was on the Thursday of that week! Impossible, of course, to go, but I was pleased to receive the invitation for I well remembered the preacher whose daughter was getting married. I had been delighted, in 1981, to know that Christian Dufour, at that time leader of the Gypsy work in India, whom I had met previously when I lived at Pool, was back again in the country, this time with a team of Indian Gypsy preachers and was willing to visit my church at Perranporth. Hastily I did some local advertising, and I had a full church to meet them and hear them sing, testify and preach, thrilling the congregation. It was one of those visiting preachers who had so kindly invited me to the wedding.

It was, of course, from India that the Gypsies had originally come to start their long trek almost around the world, and their language shows its roots in the language of that part of India from which they came. They are becoming increasingly aware of their roots in that land and fairly recently India has recognised her links with the Gypsies, some even imagining that one day they will return to that land as the Jews have returned to Israel. No wonder then that the Gypsy missionaries have long regarded India as a mission field worthy of their efforts for at least twenty million Gypsies still live in that subcontinent.

The Gypsy mission, though, was not first in the field to try to reach Indian Gypsies with the gospel. As long ago as 1940 an American Christian woman had welcomed Gypsies and talked to them of the Lord. As a result of the work of this unnamed Christian, some 10,000 of them made a profession of following Christ and, thirty years or so later, there were still hundreds of them maintaining the faith. An unnamed American woman appears later in the story. Perhaps it is the same one, for she had opened a home for Indian Gypsy children from which later emerged teachers, doctors and nurses. Apart from the individual work of this remarkable woman, the Methodist Church had also run homes for Indian Gypsy children, a work that was to prove of immense value.

The first real contact made by the Gypsy mission was in 1966 when exploratory visits were made to some areas. Le Cossec visited India in 1968, accompanying a friend as his interpreter, and with them was the preacher Jacob. They were able to make contact with Gypsies in the South of India and they discovered that news of the revival in Europe had reached India by way of American Christian reviews. It was then that Le Cossec met Christian Dufour, who had been introduced to the revival by Gypsies in France.

The work started and grew and, by 1973, the evangelist Jacob was able to report that there were now 500 Gypsies in India baptised, with eight preachers ministering to them. He had only just completed a mission among some Gypsies who lived in the desert and also at other Gypsy camps, where he was able to provide food and clothes to the converted Gypsies and their children. There were now regular Sunday morning services and also services for children in the evenings. Wednesday was Bible study night, on Saturday they fasted and had a prayer meeting, and it was the wish soon to have regular monthly communion services. About sixteen miles outside of Trichy a plot of ground had been bought, where an orphanage for Gypsy children would be built, which would also provide for their education. Quite clearly the problem of 'rice Christians' could well arise, but these Gypsies defended the missionaries who made material provision for them by claiming that the Hindu people had never come forward to help them as the Christians had done. Other problems presented themselves, for Jacob and his family suffered greatly from abuse and persecution, but still continued in their work.

By now Christian Dufour was supervising the work of the Indian evangelists and plans were afoot to establish bases in Afghanistan, Turkey, Iraq and Iran for pioneer work in the East. By 1977 the mission had worked out a plan of action for India. Its aim was dual, social and spiritual. On the social side they planned homes, schools and wells, whilst the spiritual aims were for further evangelisation and Bible training for the newly called preachers. A very promising and encouraging fruit of the work had already emerged in Salomon. In his childhood he had been placed in an evangelical home by an American woman (the same one?) who had cared for him as her own son, continuing to provide for him in college. Now he had entered the Southern Asia Bible College of the Assemblies of God. Aged twenty-three, he was embarking upon three years of study to prepare him to evangelise his own tribe of Gypsies, known in India as the Lambadis. Great was the joy of Salomon when, on a mission from college to his home village, he saw his Hindu parents give their lives to Christ.

The Salomon story came as a challenge and confirmation of the aim of the mission to start courses themselves for the Gypsy preachers, as well as to open homes for Gypsy children. Soon three were open and catering for a total of 100 children, each of whom was maintained financially by French, Finnish or Gypsy families. In some cases the childrens' families lived with them and shared their meals, such was the hunger in that area.

Visiting India again in 1978, Le Cossec found that the

thirteen schools now opened by AMET (*Action Mondiale D'Évangélisation Tzigane*) were working satisfactorily and eight preachers, who were also teachers in the schools, were now employed, as well as five women teachers and others eager to help in the work. The first Bible study course now took place at the National Gypsy Centre at Trichy, where twenty-two pupils underwent Bible teaching, as a result of which eight young Gypsies offered to serve Christ as preachers. Twelve water baptisms took place and later, in Delhi, the possibility was explored of evangelising a new tribe of the Indian Gypsies. On the practical side, it was hoped to be able to sink twenty wells. Twenty-seven preachers were being supported, of whom three were Gypsies, and a national council had been appointed to oversee the work in India under the leadership of Christian Dufour.

Tens of thousands of Gypsies had now been contacted and there were hopes for two conventions in 1979. Imagine the joy of the Gypsy preacher Daniel working with his family in a field in an isolated village when the mission van appeared totally unexpectedly! This valiant, often persecuted preacher had built a new chapel financed by gifts from Gypsies from other countries, and there were now five Gypsy families converted. Greatly encouraged by the visit, he told the visitors that he was soon off to undertake a six-month evangelistic tour of Gypsy villages. Daniel was a Gypsy from the Lambadi tribe, like Salomon. A member of another Gypsy tribe, the Narikoravas (fox-eaters!) was John. Aged twenty-one, he also had been at a Bible school for two years and was now to work among his own people. Abandoned in a train as a young boy, he had been cared for by a Gypsy preacher who had raised him with financial help from French Gypsies.

Evidence of the continuing support from the mission was seen in 1982. A poor Gypsy chief had appealed for help for the children of his tribe who only had one meal of rice a day. The generous response of the European Gypsies had now meant that they had three meals.

By 1979 more than 150 children were being cared for in the mission's homes with all the evangelistic possibilities that this affords, and the first convention had been held, when around 1,000 Gypsies of the Narikoravas tribe had gathered. This tribe was very poor and numbered tens of thousands, its men living by hunting and the women by the selling of trinkets, whilst the children begged. Here we see the negative side of the 'rice Christian' problem. Almost half of those attending left the convention after the first meeting. People outside the mission had urged them to ask the Europeans for money and, being refused, they had immediately left. For those who remained, however, it was a richly blessed experience and the convention concluded with a service of baptism. Among the fifteen baptised was a tribal chief.

The second convention gathered about 1,200 Gypsies of the Lambadi tribe. This lasted for three days and the meetings continued from seven in the morning until ten at night with breaks only for meals of rice. Here the baptisms numbered about thirty and were followed by a service for the reception of the baptism of the Holy Spirit in which God sent His Spirit on many present. Food was served free during these two conventions and more than 13,000 meals were provided, thanks to the generosity of Gypsy Christians in France, Switzerland and Belgium.

Plans were still being made for the future, including the creation of more homes for children in the North, each providing for twenty-five children, and one at Pondicherry, also for twenty-five children. There would be, it was hoped, a home for young girls, the opening of new schools and the sending of five evangelists, at the tribe's request, to the Lambadis. The wells already dug had proved their value, as was demonstrated by the sight of fields cultivated by their aid.

In 1980 another visit by Le Cossec gave him the opportunity of meeting the ten evangelists working with the Narikoravas tribe. They also visited John in his apartment, which served as his living-room, bedroom, kitchen and office. It measured three metres by two metres! Salomon told them that now the whole of his village was converted. Then there was a meeting with all the preacher/teachers and their wives as well as the women teachers in the conference room of a hotel in Hyderabad. One of the burning issues was which of their previous customs should be forbidden to Gypsies who became converted. (There was, for example, a custom that obliged a man to marry his brother's widow.)

In 1981 the growth of the work could be measured by the fact that while fifteen years before, it had started with five workers, now there were forty, three of whom were Gypsies. Of the twenty millions of Gypsies in India, 100,000 had been evangelised so there were still many millions to reach. Among those trying to reach them was Salomon, who was now engaged in translating the New Testament into the Gypsy language.

1982 brought shattering news for the mission in India. Christian Dufour and his family were expelled! He had simply been informed that their visas had not been renewed and that they had to return to France in June. This was a great blow for the family after fifteen years of service in the country. A blow, too, for the mission, but they were able to carry on, for Le Cossec had organised a council of Indian and Gypsy preachers in each state, and Dufour and others were permitted to visit India for visits of three months duration. Salomon, though, was still working and witnessing brightly. His sister was evangelising too and, by her witness and that of her family, God had saved three souls in a Gypsy village. In that year Le Cossec, accompanied by Dufour, was able to visit India again, and one of the first things he did was to appoint Salomon as President of the Gypsy mission at Tamil Nadu, and the success of this young man inspired an appeal for funds to help people adopt children, as he had been adopted. It must have been a great occasion when Le Cossec was able to have a meal with the American woman who had adopted Salomon. For years she had lived in the most remote part of India, telling people of Christ, and had founded several Christian churches. Now she was eighty-two, still active and still using her jeep to visit villages. To visit Salomon's village she had walked fifteen kilometres through a forest!

Seventeen schools were now built, catering for 750. Now, for the first time, a national convention for preachers from the whole of India was held. It was agreed that church buildings were now needed in fifteen villages and it was reported that 1500 Gypsies were now baptised from the Narikoracas tribe, and 500 from the Lambadis. In the absence of Dufour, an Indian pastor, Selvaraj, was placed in charge of the whole work. As a result of this visit an appeal was launched in 1983 for money for churches, as well as autocycles and bicycles for the evangelists. The same year saw the growth of the work in various parts and the money from the appeal sufficed to build four churches, buy two autocycles and one bicycle, as well as finance for the sinking of a well.

By the following year, with the help of the German Gypsy mission, there was money for more bicycles and autocycles, the purchase of land for the future Bible School and the start of its construction. The money also provided for one children's home, three teachers and the sinking of another well, the repair of roofs damaged in a storm and a new church building. Three more preachers were to be supported and the preachers now would have greater opportunity to preach, as their responsibility for work in the childrens' homes would be decreased. They would be replaced by deacons, as in the Acts of the Apostles. There were acts of the apostles, indeed, in this, the homeland of the Gypsies!

Concluding Thoughts

Gypsy children out selling sweets so that their father could go to the Bible School and train as a preacher; Gypsy chaplains in prisons; a Gypsy radio programme beaming out the gospel all over Europe; these and other stories could have been told about this remarkable movement and its past. The movement has not been without its critics. It has been suggested that it is a kind of religious projection of Gypsy self-consciousness and is largely nationalistic. Certainly I feel the movement needs to remember that even greater revivals have taken place in the past without the miraculous element that this movement so greatly values. Whatever one may say, though, it is undoubtedly a mighty work of God. What of its future?

As young Gypsies, increasingly literate, begin to think deeply about the Bible and Christian history, there are bound to be those who will find it impossible to accept many of the tenets and practices of the present movement. The movement could change to cater for them, but I doubt if it will. My own forecast is that it will increasingly seek to be connected with the parent Pentecostal movement and some of its brightest young people will leave. This though will not prove to be a disaster. I well remember a lecturer commenting on how a famous English literary family was revitalised when one of its children married a Gypsy. The Gypsy blood brought new zest to a highly-bred and somewhat refined family. So, when the Gypsy Christians come, in ever-increasing numbers into the main churches, they will bring new vitality, a breath of fresh air we so much need, and perhaps this will be among the greatest of the benefits that the great Gypsy revival will have bestowed.